Tests and Measurement
in Early Childhood Education

SUE CLARK WORTHAM
The University of Texas at San Antonio

MERRILL PUBLISHING COMPANY
A Bell & Howell Information Company
Columbus   Toronto   London   Melbourne

Published by Merrill Publishing Company
A Bell & Howell Information Company
Columbus, Ohio 43216

This book was set in Palatino.

Administrative Editor: David Faherty
Production Coordinator: Mary Irvin
Art Coordinator: Lorraine Woost
Cover Designer: Brian Deep

Library of Congress Catalog Card Number: 89–61879
International Standard Book Number: 0–675–20665–0
Printed in the United States of America

1 2 3 4 5 6 7 8 9—94 93 92 91 90

Preface

All students who are preparing to become elementary school teachers take a course in tests and measurements as part of their undergraduate curriculum. Many textbooks for such courses describe both psychological and teacher-designed tests and how they are used to assess and evaluate students.

Students who are preparing to become teachers of young children, those from prekindergarten through the primary grades, must be prepared to measure or evaluate children who are in the period of development called *early childhood*. Tests and other measurements designed for young children are different from those intended for children in elementary and secondary schools. Because infants and children under age 8 have developmental limitations and differences from older children, a textbook that discusses measurement and evaluation in the early childhood years must be written from a developmental perspective.

This book is written especially for teachers and future teachers of young children. It includes not only information about standardized tests used in the early childhood years, but also about other types of evaluation and measurement that are developmentally appropriate for younger children, such as observation, checklists and rating scales, and tests designed by teachers.

An important factor in the measurement of young children is when and how they should be tested and evaluated. This is a controversial issue. The strengths and weaknesses of each type of measurement presented are discussed, as well as research on the problems surrounding testing and evaluation in early childhood.

The book is divided into two parts. The first half is devoted to topics about standardized tests. Following an introductory chapter that gives the historical background of measurement and evaluation in early childhood and an overview of different types of measurement used with young children, the next three chapters discuss standardized tests. Chapter 2 describes the differences between standardized tests and informal evaluation measures. Chapter 3 provides information on the process of designing standardized tests, and Chapter 4 discusses how these tests are used with young children.

Informal methods of evaluating children are covered beginning with Chapter 5. Observation as a measurement tool is described in this chapter, and checklists and rating scales are discussed in Chapter 6. The ways that teachers design their own assessments in early childhood classes are related to the developmental level of their students. Chapter 7 describes how concrete, hands-on assessment tasks are gradually replaced by paper-and-pencil activities as students achieve some competence in reading and writing.

Chapter 8, the final chapter of the book, looks ahead. Early childhood education is in a period of growth. As more children are taught at younger ages in various types of programs, the need to measure their progress will increase the requirement for appropriate measurement tools. The programs that serve young children must also be evaluated. The design and improvement of developmentally appropriate measurements to be used with these children will be an important consideration in future decades.

This book was initiated at the suggestion of undergraduate students enrolled in a course in tests and measurements in early childhood. Over a period of 2 years, these students worked with tentative materials and initial drafts, providing feedback on content and format.

A group of graduate students gave generously of their time and expertise during development of the final draft. Special thanks are due to Sharron Calhoun, Cynthia Cates, Susan Fillinger, Marla MacDonald, Della Meyer, Mary Jo Nelson, Nancy Pfrang, Linda Williams, and Cheryl Workman, who spent many hours studying and discussing each chapter.

I would like to thank the reviewers who provided valuable suggestions and feedback during the writing process. Their input has helped to make this a better book, and I am indebted to them for their assistance. Those who reviewed parts or all of the manuscript are Richard Fiene, Pennsylvania State University–Harrisburg; Darla Springate, Eastern Kentucky University; Tes Mehring, Emporia State University; Susan Kontos, Purdue University; John Johnston, Memphis State University; Ronald Padula, Delaware County Community College; Landace Logan, Emporia State University; and Ruth Hough, Georgia State University.

I would also like to thank Dave Faherty, editor at Merrill Publishing Company, for helping me struggle through the inevitable changes and modifications that must be made as a book evolves.

Sue Wortham

Contents

2
Strategies for Measurement and Evaluation   13

3
Standardized Tests   31

4
Using and Reporting Standardized Test Results   59

5
Informal Evaluation Measures: Observation   83

7
Informal Measures: Classroom and Teacher Designed Tests and Assessments   133

8
Putting Measurement and Evaluation in
Perspective: Looking Ahead   159

Appendix: A Selected Annotated
Bibliography of Evaluation Instruments for
Infancy and Early Childhood   173

Glossary   177

Index   181

List of Figures

1

An Overview of Measurement and Evaluation in Early Childhood

Throughout elementary and high school, children take many different kinds of tests. Some tests determine their grades for each reporting period; some are achievement tests, IQ tests, and tests for admission to a college or university. However, measurement and evaluation is more than the testing that is familiar to us. Furthermore, we may be unaware of the role that measurement and evaluation plays with children in the years from birth to 8 years of age.

Measurement can mean many things. Goodwin and Goodwin (1982) described measurement as "the process of determining, through observation or testing, an individual's traits or behaviors, a program's characteristics, or the properties of some other entity, and then assigning a number, rating, or score to that determination" (p. 523). The studying of individuals for measurement purposes begins before birth with assessments of fetal growth and development. At birth and throughout infancy and early childhood, various methods of measurement are used to evaluate the individual's traits or behaviors. Before a child is able to take a written test, he is measured through medical examinations, observation of developmental milestones by parents and other family members, and perhaps screened or evaluated for an early childhood program or service.

Information about measurement, particularly for psychological testing, comes from many sources. All college students preparing to become teachers take

EARLY INTERVENTION FOR A HEARING-IMPAIRED CHILD

Julio, who is 2 years old, was born prematurely. He did not have regular checkups during his first year, but was taken by his mother to a community clinic when he had a cold and fever at about 9 months of age.

When she noticed that Julio did not react to normal sounds in the examining room, the clinic doctor stood behind him and clapped her hands near each ear. Because Julio did not turn toward the clapping sounds, the doctor suspected that he had a hearing loss. She arranged for Julio to be examined by an audiologist at an eye, ear, nose, and throat clinic.

Julio was found to have a significant hearing loss in both ears. He was fitted with hearing aids and is attending a special program twice a week for children with hearing deficits. Therapists in the program are teaching Julio to speak. They are also teaching his mother how to make Julio aware of his surroundings and help him develop a vocabulary. Had Julio not received intervention services at an early age, he might have entered school with severe cognitive and learning deficits that would have put him at a higher risk for learning.

courses in educational psychology in which they learn about the characteristics of various tests, how they are administered, and how the results are interpreted.

How is a book on measurement and evaluation of young children different from textbooks prepared for courses in educational psychology? Most textbooks in testing and measurement focus primarily on the psychological and educational testing of school-age children and adults, with some attention to younger individuals. The tests and teacher assessments described usually assume some facility in reading and writing.

Measurement of children from birth through the preschool years is different from measurement of older people. Not only can young children not write or read, but the young developing child presents different challenges that influence the choice of measurement strategy. Evaluation strategies must be matched to the level of mental, social, and physical development at each stage. Developmental change in young children is rapid, and there is a need to assess whether development is progressing normally. If development is not normal, measurement and evaluation procedures used are important in making decisions regarding appropriate intervention services during infancy and the preschool years.

If medical problems, birth defects, or developmental delays in motor, language, cognitive, or social development are discovered during the early, critical periods of development, steps can be taken to correct, minimize, or remediate them before the child enters school. For many developmental deficits or differences, the earlier they are detected and the earlier intervention is planned, the more likely the child will be able to overcome them or compensate for them. For example, if a serious hearing deficit is identified early, the child can learn other methods of communicating and acquiring information.

Besides identifying and correcting developmental problems, measurement of very young children is conducted for other purposes. One purpose is research.

Researchers study young children to understand their behavior better or to meas-ure the appropriateness of the experiences that are provided for them.

Measurement of young children is also used to place them in infant or early childhood programs or to provide special services. To make sure that a child receives the best services, careful screening and more extensive testing may be conducted before selecting the combination of intervention programs and other services that will best serve the child.

Program planning is another purpose of measurement. When children have been identified and evaluated for an intervention program or service, measure-ment results can also be used in planning the programs that will serve them. These programs, in turn, can be evaluated to determine their effectiveness.

How were these measurement strategies developed? The next section de-scribes how certain movements or factors, especially during this century, have affected the development of testing instruments, procedures, and other measure-ment techniques that are used with infants and young children.

THE EVOLUTION OF MEASUREMENT AND TESTING WITH YOUNG CHILDREN

Interest in studying young children to understand their growth and development dates back to the initial recognition of childhood as a separate period in the life cycle. Johann Pestalozzi, a pioneer in developing educational programs specifi-cally for children, wrote about the development of his three-and-a-half-year-old son in 1774 (Irwin & Bushnell, 1980). Early publications also reflected concern for the proper upbringing and education of young children. *Some Thoughts Concerning Education* by John Locke (1693), *Emile* (Rousseau, 1762), and Frederick Froebel's *Education of Man* (1826) were influential in focusing attention on the characteristics and needs of children in the eighteenth and nineteenth centuries. Rousseau believed that human nature was essentially good and that education must allow that goodness to unfold. He stated that more attention should be given to studying the child so that education could be adapted to meet individual needs (Weber, 1984). The study of children, as advocated by Rousseau, did not begin until the late nineteenth and early twentieth centuries.

Scientists throughout the world used observation to measure human behav-iors. Ivan Pavlov proposed a theory of conditioning. Alfred Binet developed the concept of a normal mental age by studying memory, attention, and intelligence in children. Binet and Theophile Simon developed an intelligence scale to deter-mine mental age that made it possible to differentiate the abilities of individual children (Weber, 1984). American psychologists expanded these early efforts, developing instruments for various types of measurement.

The study and measurement of young children today has evolved from the child study movement, the development of standardized tests, Head Start and other federal programs funded in the 1960s, and the passage of Public Law 94-142 to better educate children with special needs. All of these movements have generated an interest in measurement or evaluation of young children and have contributed to the development of tests and measures designed specifically for this age group.

The Child Study Movement

G. Stanley Hall, Charles Darwin, and Lawrence Frank were leaders in the development of this child study movement that emerged after the turn of the century. Darwin, in suggesting that by studying the development of the infant one could glimpse the development of the human species, initiated the scientific study of the child (Kessen, 1965). Hall developed and extended methods of studying children. When he became president of Clark University, he established a major center for child study. Hall's students, John Dewey, Arnold Gesell, and Lewis Terman, all made major contributions to the study and measurement of children. John Dewey advocated educational reform that affected the development of educational programs for young children. Arnold Gesell first described the behaviors that emerged in children at each chronological age, and Terman became a leader in the development of mental tests (Irwin & Bushnell, 1980).

Research in child rearing and child care was furthered by the establishment of the Laura Spelman Rockefeller Memorial child development grants. Under the leadership of Lawrence Frank, institutes for child development were funded by the Rockefeller grants at Columbia University's Teachers College, the University of Minnesota, the University of California at Berkeley, Arnold Gesell's Clinic of Child Development at Yale, the Iowa Child Welfare Station, and other locations.

With the establishment of child study at academic centers, preschool children could be observed in group settings, rather than as individuals in the home. With the development of laboratory schools and nursery schools in the home economic departments of colleges and universities, child study research could also include the family in broadening the understanding of child development. Researchers from many disciplines joined in an ongoing child study movement that originated strategies for observing and measuring development. The results of their research led to an abundant literature. Between the 1890s and the 1950s, hundreds of children were studied in academic settings throughout the United States (Weber, 1984). Thus the child study movement has taught us how to use observation and other strategies to measure the child. Investigators today continue to add new knowledge about child development and learning that aids parents, preschool teachers and staff members, and professionals in institutions and agencies that provide services to children and families (Irwin & Bushnell, 1980).

Standardized Tests

Standardized testing also began around 1900. When colleges and universities in the East sought applicants from other areas of the nation in the 1920s, they found the high school transcripts of these students difficult to evaluate. The Scholastic

Aptitude Test was established to permit fairer comparisons of applicants seeking admission (Cronbach, 1984).

As public schools expanded to offer 12 years of education, a similar phenomenon occurred. To determine the level of instruction, pace of instruction, and grouping of students without regard for socioeconomic class, objective tests were developed (Gardner, 1961). These tests grew out of the need to sort, select, or otherwise make decisions about both children and adults.

The first efforts to design tests were informal. When a psychologist, researcher, or physician needed a method to observe a behavior, he developed a procedure to meet his needs. The procedure was often adopted by others with the same needs. When many people wanted to use a particular measurement strategy or test, the developer prepared printed copies for sale. As the demand for tests grew, textbook publishers and firms specializing in test development and production also began to create and/or sell tests (Cronbach, 1984).

American psychologists built upon the work of Binet and Simon in developing the intelligence measures described earlier. Binet's instrument, revised by Terman at Stanford University, came to be known as the *Stanford-Binet Intelligence Scale*. Other Americans, particularly educators, welcomed the opportunity to use precise measurements to evaluate learning. Edward Thorndike and his students designed measures to evaluate achievement in reading, mathematics, spelling, and language ability (Weber, 1984). By 1918 there were over 100 standardized tests designed to measure school achievement (Monroe, 1918).

After World War II the demand for dependable and technically refined tests grew, and people of all ages came to be tested. As individuals and institutions selected and developed their own tests, the use of testing became more centralized. Statewide tests were administered in schools, and tests were increasingly used at the national level.

The expanded use of tests resulted in the establishment of giant corporations that could assemble the resources to develop, publish, score, and report the results of testing to a large clientele. Centralization improved the quality of tests and the establishment of standards for test design. As individual researchers and teams of psychologists continue to design instruments to meet current needs, the high quality of these newer tests can be attributed to the improvements and refinements made over the years and to increased knowledge of test design and validation (Cronbach, 1984).

Head Start and the War on Poverty

Prior to the 1960s, tests for preschool children were developed for use by medical doctors, psychologists, and other professionals serving children. Developmental measures, IQ tests, and specialized tests to measure developmental deficits were generally used for noneducational purposes. Child study researchers tended to use observational or unobtrusive methods to study the individual child or groups of children. School-age children were tested to measure school achievement, but this type of test was rarely used with preschool children.

When the federal government decided to improve the academic performance of lower-class children and those from non-English-speaking backgrounds, test developers moved quickly to develop new measurement and evaluation instruments for these preschool and school-age populations.

In the late 1950s, there was a growing concern about the consistently low academic performance of children from poor homes. As researchers began to investigate the problem, national interest in improving education led to massive funding for many programs designed to reduce the disparity in achievement between poor and middle-class children. The major program that involved preschool children was Head Start. Models of early childhood programs ranging from highly structured academic, child-centered developmental to more traditional nursery school models were designed and implemented throughout the United States (White, 1973; Zigler & Valentine, 1979).

All programs funded by the federal government had to be evaluated for effectiveness. As a result, new measures were developed to assess individual progress and their effectiveness (Laosa, 1982). The quality of these measures was uneven, as were comparative research designs to compare the overall effectiveness of Head Start. Nevertheless, the measures and strategies developed for use with Head Start projects added valuable resources for the assessment and evaluation of young children (Hoepfner, Stern, & Nummedal, 1971).

Other federally funded programs developed in the 1960s, such as bilingual programs, Title I, Emergency School Aid Act, Follow Through, and Home Start, were similar in effect to Head Start. The need for measurement strategies and tests to evaluate these programs led to the improvement of existing tests and the development of new tests to evaluate their success accurately.

PL 94-142: Mainstreaming Young Handicapped Children

Perhaps the most significant law affecting the measurement of children was Public Law (PL) 94-142, passed in 1975. This law guaranteed all handicapped children the right to an appropriate education in a free public school and placement in the least restrictive learning environment. The law further required the use of nondiscriminatory testing and evaluation of these children (Mehrens & Lehmann, 1984).

The implications of the law were far-reaching. Testing, identification, and placement of mentally retarded students and those with other handicapping conditions were difficult. Existing tests were no longer considered adequate for children with special needs. Classroom teachers had to learn the techniques used to identify handicapped students and determine how to meet their educational needs (Kaplan & Saccuzzo, 1982).

The law requires that a team of teachers, parents, diagnosticians, school psychologists, medical personnel, and perhaps social workers or representatives of government agencies or institutions be used to identify and place handicapped students. When appropriate, the child must also be included in the decision-making process. The team screens, tests, and develops an individual educational

ONE FAMILY'S EXPERIENCE WITH HEAD START

R osa is a graduate of the Head Start program. For 2 years she participated in a class housed in the James Brown School, a former inner-city school that had been closed and re-modeled for other community services. There were two Head Start classrooms in the building, which was shared with several other community agencies serving low-income families. In addition to learning at James Brown School, Rosa went on many field trips to places including the zoo, the botanical garden, the public library, and a nearby McDonald's.

This year Rosa is a kindergarten student at West Oaks Elementary School with her older brothers, who also attended Head Start. Next year Rosa's younger sister Luisa will begin the program. Luisa looks forward to Head Start. She has good memories of the things she observed Rosa doing in the Head Start classroom while visiting the school with her mother.

Luisa's parents are also happy that she will be attending the Head Start program. Luisa's older brothers are good students, which they attribute to the background they received in Head Start. From her work in kindergarten, it appears that Rosa will also do well when she enters first grade.

program for each child. Not all team members are involved in every step of the process, but they can influence the decisions made.

The term *mainstreaming* came to define the requirement that the child be placed in the least restrictive environment. This meant that as often as possible the child would be placed with nonhandicapped children, rather than in a seg-regated classroom for special education students. How much mainstreaming is beneficial for the individual student? The question has not yet been answered. In addition, the ability of teachers to meet the needs of handicapped and nonhan-dicapped students simultaneously in the same classroom is still debated. Never-theless, classroom teachers are expected to develop and monitor the educational program prescribed for special education students (Clark, 1976).

The identification and diagnosis of handicapped students is the most com-plex aspect of PL 94-142. Many different types of children need special education, including the mentally retarded, the physically and visually handicapped, the speech impaired, the hard-of-hearing and deaf, the learning disabled, the emo-tionally disturbed, and the gifted. Children may have a combination of handicap-ping conditions. The identification and comprehensive testing of children to determine what types of handicap they have and how best to educate them requires a vast array of measurement techniques and instruments. Teachers, school nurses, and other staff members can be involved in initial screening and referral, but the extensive testing used for diagnosis and prescription requires professionals who have been trained to administer psychological tests (Mehrens & Lehmann, 1984).

Under PL 94-142, all handicapped children between the ages of 3 and 21 are entitled to free public education. This means that preschool programs must also be provided for children under the age of 6. Public schools have implemented early childhood programs for handicapped children, and Head Start programs are required to include them (Guralnick, 1982). Other institutions and agencies also provide preschool programs for handicapped and nonhandicapped children.

Meeting the developmental and educational needs of preschool handicapped children, and at the same time providing mainstreaming, is a complex task. How should these children be grouped for the best intervention services? When handicapped and nonhandicapped children are grouped together, what are the effects when all of them are progressing through critical periods of development? Not only is identification of preschool handicapped children more complex, but evaluation of the preschool programs providing intervention services is difficult (Allen, 1980; Bronfenbrenner, 1975).

Many of the shortcomings of PL 94-142 were addressed in PL 99-457, passed in 1986. The newer law authorized two new programs, the Federal Preschool Program and the Early Intervention Program. Under PL 94-142, the state could choose whether to provide services to handicapped children between the ages of 3 and 5. Under PL 99-457, states must prove that they are meeting the needs of all of these children if they wish to receive federal funds under PL 94-142. The Federal Preschool Program extends the rights of handicapped children under PL 94-142 to all handicapped children between the ages of 3 and 5.

The Early Intervention Program established early intervention services for all children between birth and 2 years of age who are developmentally delayed. At the end of the 5-year implementation period, participating states must provide intervention services for all handicapped infants and toddlers (Morrison, 1988).

How to measure and evaluate young handicapped children and the programs that serve them is a continuing challenge (Guralnick, 1982). The design of measures to screen, identify, and place preschool children in intervention programs began with the passage of PL 94-142 and was extended under PL 99-457. Many of these instruments and strategies, particularly those dealing with developmental delay, are now also used with preschool programs serving normal children, as well as those with developmental delays or handicaps.

CURRENT PRACTICES AND TRENDS IN MEASUREMENT AND EVALUATION IN EARLY CHILDHOOD EDUCATION

The 1980s brought a new reform movement in education accompanied by a new emphasis on testing. The effort to improve education at all levels included the use of standardized tests to provide accountability for what students are learning. Minimum competency tests, achievement tests, and screening instruments were used to ensure that students from preschool through college reached the desired educational goals and achieved the minimum standards of education that were established locally or by the state education agency.

The increased use of testing at all levels has been criticized, but the testing of young children is of particular concern. Standardized tests and other informal measures are now being used in preschool, kindergarten, and first grade to decide whether children will be admitted to preschool programs, promoted to first grade or placed in a transitional classroom, or retained. Those who advocate raising standards in education are calling for more stringent policies to improve school achievement. The use of tests with young children for placement purposes has serious implications because it can be developmentally inappropriate for this age group. Decisions made about placement, particularly placement in a transitional class or retention in a grade, can have a strong impact on the self-esteem of young children, particularly their perception of whether they are successful students or failures.

Although early childhood specialists, both individuals and organizations, are concerned about the trends in education and testing of young children, developmentally inappropriate practices continue to expand. Now more than ever, teachers, parents, and other adults active in the care and education of young children need to be informed about the measurement of these children and when and how it should be conducted. This textbook is such a resource.

AN OVERVIEW OF TOPICS COVERED IN THIS BOOK

In the chapters that follow, measurement and evaluation are discussed in terms of how they are applied to infants and young children. Basic information is provided about each topic in general, and then the application of the information to young children is explained. Issues regarding each topic are also explored. Thus, the background information needed to understand a facet of measurement is presented, as well as the pertinence of the measurement approach when used with young children.

Chapter 2, "Introduction to Measurement and Evaluation," introduces the types of measurement that will be presented in later chapters. This chapter briefly discusses the categories of measurement and evaluation strategies used with infants and preschool children and explains why they are used. The strategies are divided into formal, or psychological, tests and informal strategies that include observation, teacher-designed measures, and checklists.

Chapter 3, "Standardized Tests," describes how standardized tests are designed. People who use these tests must know how they should be constructed and pilot-tested before they are made available to the public. Administration and interpretation of test scores is also covered. Many issues surround the use of standardized tests, particularly with young children. These issues are explained in a discussion of the advantages and disadvantages of using such tests with young children. Also provided are suggestions on how standardized tests should be evaluated and selected. The reader is directed to strategies for determining the quality of these tests by studying the test manual and reading reviews of the test in test review resources.

Standardized tests can be classified as having norm-referenced results, criterion-referenced results, or both. Chapter 4, "Using and Reporting Standardized

Test Results," discusses the distinctions between the two types of tests and how each is used with young children. An important part of test administration and interpretation is knowing how to share the information about test results. Teachers must know how to report a child's performance to parents, while school district personnel must report school and district results to school staff, administrators, and the board of education. The advantages and disadvantages of using criterion-referenced and norm-referenced tests are also included.

In Chapter 5, "Informal Evaluation Measures: Observation," the focus shifts from standardized tests to informal means of evaluation. These informal methods are reviewed before we explore the types of observation that can be done to learn about the child's development and behavior. The role of observation in understanding specific areas of development is explained to include physical, social and emotional, cognitive, and language development. Many strengths and weaknesses are inherent in the use of observation. These are discussed, and guidelines for observation are suggested.

Checklists and rating scales are instruments that can be used for evaluation purposes. In Chapter 6, "Informal Measures: Checklists and Rating Scales," appropriate uses are described. Because checklists also have other purposes, the discussion of their design and use indicates how they can be used as a guide to understand development, to develop curriculum, and to evaluate learning development. The process of checklist design is explained, as well as the strengths and limitations of checklists as measurement and evaluation resources.

The final type of informal measure is discussed in Chapter 7, "Informal Measures: Classroom/Teacher-Designed Tests and Assessments." Because teacher-conducted assessments designed for preschool children must be task oriented, rather than a pencil-and-paper activity, each of these measures is discussed separately. The design of a teacher-conducted evaluation includes designing test objectives, constructing a table of specifications, organizing the instrument or tasks, and providing for instruction and extensions and correctives.

Finally, Chapter 8, "Putting Measurement and Evaluation in Perspective: Looking Ahead," provides a synthesis of the problems and opportunities involved in the evaluation and assessment of young children. The use of early childhood measures for program evaluation, and the importance and process of program evaluation, are discussed as an extension of the measurement of children. Because we are in a period of new influences and directions in early childhood education, measurement and evaluation strategies are again in the forefront in evaluating the effectiveness of schooling. Ongoing issues are discussed, as well as the trends that developed as the 1980s drew to a close.

REFERENCES

Allen, K. E. (1980). Mainstreaming: What have we learned? *Young Children, 35,* 54–63.

Bronfenbrenner, U. (1975). Is early intervention effective? In B. Z. Friedlander, G. M. Sterritt, & G. E. Kirk (Eds.), *Exceptional Infant* (Vol. 2). New York: Bruner/Mazel.

Clark, E. A. (1976). Teacher attitudes toward integration of children with handicaps. *Education and Training of the Mentally Retarded, 11,* 333–335.

Cronbach, L. J. (1984). *Essentials of psychological testing.* New York: Harper & Row.

Froebel, F. (1896). *Education of man.* New York: Appleton.

Gardner, J. W. (1961). *Excellence: Can we be equal and excellent too?* New York: Harper & Row.

Goodwin, W. L., & Goodwin, L. D. (1982). Measuring young children. In B. Spodek (Ed.), *Handbook of research in early childhood education.* New York: Free Press.

Guralnick, M. J. (1982). Mainstreaming young handicapped children: A public policy and ecological systems analysis. In B. Spodek (Ed.), *Handbook of research in early childhood education* (pp. 456–500). New York: Free Press.

Hoepfner, R., Stern, C., & Nummedal, S. (Eds.). (1971). *CSE-ECRC preschool/kindergarten test evaluations.* Los Angeles: UCLA Graduate School of Education.

Irwin, D. M., & Bushnell, M. M. (1980). *Observational strategies for child study.* New York: Holt, Rinehart and Winston.

Kaplan, R. M., & Saccuzzo, D. P. (1982). *Psychological testing principles: Applications and issues.* Monterrey, CA: Brooks/Cole.

Kessen, W. (1965). *The child.* New York: Wiley.

Laosa, L. M. (1982). The sociocultural context of evaluation. In B. Spodek (Ed.), *Handbook of research in early childhood education* (pp. 501–520). New York: Free Press.

Locke, J. (1699). *Some thoughts concerning education* (4th ed., enlarged). London: A & J Churchill.

Mehrens, W. A., & Lehmann, I. J. (1984). *Measurement and evaluation in education and psychology* (3rd ed.). New York: Holt, Rinehart and Winston.

Monroe, W. S. (1918). Existing tests and standards. In G. W. Whipple (Ed.), *The measurement of educational products, 14th yearbook of the National Society for the Study of Education, Part II* (pp. 71–104). Bloomington, IL: Public School Publishing Co.

Morrison, G. S. (1988). *Educational development of infants, toddlers, and preschoolers.* Glenview, IL: Scott, Foresman.

Rousseau, J. J. (1911). *Emile or On education* (B. Foxley, trans.). London: Dent.

Weber, E. (1984). *Ideas influencing early childhood education. A theoretical analysis.* New York: Teachers College Press.

White, S. H. (1973). *Federal programs for young children: Review and recommendations* (Vols. 1–3). Washington, DC: U.S. Government Printing Office.

Zigler, E., & Valentine, J. (Eds.). (1979). *Project Head Start: A legacy of the War on Poverty.* New York: Free Press.

2
Strategies for Measurement and Evaluation

What are measurement and evaluation? Why do we need to test or evaluate children in the early childhood years?

We live in a world where we are interested not only in knowing more about how infants and young children grow and develop but also in having access to tools to help us with problems in a child's development and learning.

Measurement and evaluation are used for various purposes. We may want to learn about individual children. We may conduct an evaluation to measure a young child's development in language or mathematics. When we need to learn more, we may assess the child to describe what she has achieved. For example, a preschool teacher may use measurement techniques to assess what concepts a child has learned prior to entering school. Likewise, a student in first grade might be assessed in reading to determine what reading skills have been mastered and what weaknesses exist that indicate a need for additional instruction.

Evaluation strategies may be used for diagnosis. Just as a medical doctor conducts a physical examination of a child to diagnose an illness, psychologists, teachers, and other adults who work with children can conduct an informal or formal assessment to diagnose a developmental delay or identify causes for poor performance in learning.

ASSESSMENT FOR RISK IN DEVELOPMENTAL STATUS

When Sarah was 6 months old, her teenage mother gave her up for adoption. Because Sarah's father could not be located to agree to release her for adoption, Sarah was placed temporarily in a foster home.

Prior to placement with the foster family, Sarah had lived with her mother in her maternal grandparents' home. In addition to Sarah's mother, there were six other children in the family. Both grandparents were employed. Sarah's primary caregiver had been a mentally retarded aunt who was 12 years old.

For the first few days after Sarah was placed in the foster home, she cried when the foster parents tried to feed her. She sat for long periods of time and stared vacantly without reacting to toys or people. She had no established patterns for sleeping and usually fretted off and on during the night.

When Sarah was examined by a pediatrician, she was found to be malnourished, with sores in her mouth from vitamin deficiencies. As determined by the Denver Developmental Screening Test, she was developing much more slowly than normal.

A special diet and multivitamins were prescribed for Sarah. Members of the foster family patiently taught her to enjoy eating a varied diet beyond the chocolate milk and cereal that she had been fed previously. Regular times for sleeping at night gradually replaced her erratic sleeping habits. Her foster family spent many hours playing with her, talking to her, and introducing her to various toys.

By the age of 11 months, Sarah had improved greatly. She was alert, ate well, began to walk, and said a few words. Her development was within the normal range, and she was ready for adoption.

Sarah had benefited from being placed in a home where she received good nutrition, guidance in living patterns, and stimulation for cognitive, physical, and social development. Without early intervention, Sarah's delay in development might have become more serious over time. Adaptability to an adoptive home might have been difficult for her and her adoptive parents. If she had been unable to adjust successfully with an adoptive family, she might have spent her childhood years in a series of foster homes, rather than with her adoptive family. She also would have been at risk for learning, beginning in the first years of schooling.

We also perform measurement and evaluation to gain information about groups of children or the success of programs or other services provided to them. Both formal and informal evaluation techniques may be used to measure a day care or preschool program that serves handicapped children. Program providers may want to know how the children in the program have benefited from the intervention services they have received. A common example of evaluation of groups of children is standardized achievement tests that are given annually by school districts. In addition to learning about the achievement of each student tested, the school district can evaluate the instructional program by studying group achievement results. Program evaluators can study group results to find areas of strength or weakness in the curriculum at different grade levels.

Just as there are many reasons for measuring and evaluating young children, various methods are also available to accomplish our goals. Sometimes we measure the child informally. We might look for characteristics by watching the child's behaviors at play or in a setting that has been arranged for that purpose. A pediatrician may watch a baby walk during an examination to determine if she is progressing normally. In a similar fashion, a teacher may observe a child playing to determine how she is using language. A second-grade teacher who constructs a set of subtraction problems to evaluate whether his students have mastered a mathematics objective is also using an **informal test.**

Formal methods or standardized instruments are also used for measurement and evaluation. These are more extensive and proven measures for evaluation. Specialists in tests and measurements design and try out instruments that evaluate the characteristics we have targeted with a large number of children. This ensures that they can use the information gained each time the test is given to another child or group of children. This type of test is called a **standardized test** because a standard has been set from the results achieved by using the test with children who are representative of the population.

Why are we interested in measuring infants and young children? The most common purpose is to assess development. Soon after birth, the **obstetrician** or **pediatrician** does an evaluation of the newborn, using the *Apgar Scale* (Apgar, 1975) to determine if it is in good health. Thereafter, at regular intervals, parents, doctors, and teachers follow the baby's development, using tests and informal evaluation strategies (Wodrich, 1984).

But what if development is not progressing normally? How can evaluation measures be used to help the young child? In recent years, researchers, medical specialists, and educators have learned how to work with children at increasingly younger ages to minimize the effects of delays in growth or other problems that retard the child's developmental progress. Various strategies and instruments are now available. A **neonatologist** conducts a comprehensive evaluation on a premature baby to determine what therapy should be initiated to improve the infant's chances for survival and optimal development. A young child can be tested for hearing loss or mental retardation. The child who does not speak normally or is late in speaking is referred to a speech pathologist, who assesses the child's language and prescribes activities to facilitate improved language development.

During infancy and the toddler years, child development specialists follow the child's progress and initiate therapy when development is not normal. During the preschool years, this effort includes evaluating and predicting whether the child is likely to experience difficulties in learning. Tests and other measures are used to determine whether the child will develop a **learning disability** and how that disability will affect her success in school. Again, when problems are detected, plans are made to work with the child in a timely manner to help her overcome as much of the disability as possible before entering school. The child may have a vision problem, difficulty in hearing, or a disability that may interfere with learning to read. The evaluation measures used will assist in identifying the exact nature of the problem. In addition, test results will be used to determine what kind of intervention will be most successful (Wodrich, 1984).

In the preschool period or even earlier, a different kind of developmental difference may emerge. Parents or other adults who deal with the child may

COMBATTING LIMITATIONS IN VOCABULARY AND CONCEPT DEVELOPMENT

Micah, who is 4 years old, is the sixth child in a family of seven children. Both of his parents work, and he and his younger brother are cared for by a grandmother during the day. Although Micah's parents are warm and loving, their combined income is barely enough to provide the basic necessities for the family. They are unable to buy books and toys that will enhance Micah's development. Because the family rarely travels outside the immediate neighborhood, Micah has had few experiences that would broaden his knowledge of the larger community.

Fortunately, Micah's family lives in a state that provides a program for 4-year-old children who can benefit from a prekindergarten class that stresses language and cognitive development. The program serves all children who come from low-income homes or exhibit language or cognitive delay.

In response to a letter sent by the school district, Micah's grandmother took him to the school to be tested for the program. Micah's performance on the test showed that he uses a limited expressive vocabulary and lacks many basic concepts. When school begins in late August, Micah will start school with his older brothers and sisters and will be enrolled in the prekindergarten class.

Micah will have the opportunity to play with puzzles, construction toys, and other manipulative objects that will facilitate his cognitive development. Stories will be read and discussed each day, and Micah will be able to look at a variety of books. Micah's teacher will introduce learning experiences that will allow Micah to learn about shapes, colors, numbers, and many other concepts that will provide a foundation for learning in the elementary school grades.

Micah will also travel with his classmates to visit places that will help him learn about the community. They may visit a furniture or grocery store or a bread factory. Visitors to the classroom will add to the students' knowledge about occupations and cultures represented in the community. The children will have opportunities to paint, participate in cooking experiences, and talk about the new things they are learning. They will dictate stories about their experiences and learn many songs and games. When Micah enters kindergarten the following year, he will use the knowledge and language he learned in prekindergarten to help him learn successfully along with his 5-year-old peers.

observe that the child demonstrates a learning ability or potential that is much higher than the normal range. A more formal evaluation using a standardized test may confirm these informal observations. Plans can then be made to facilitate the child's development to help her achieve her full potential for learning.

Although potential for learning may be assessed at a very early age in the gifted or talented child, learning aptitude may also be evaluated in the general population during the preschool and primary school years. Educators wish to determine children's learning abilities and needs, as well as the type of program that will be most beneficial for them. Informal strategies and formal tests are used with individual children and groups of children to assess what and how much they have already learned previously and to evaluate weak areas that can be given special attention. Informal and formal strategies are also used to evaluate the success of programs that serve children, as well as provide indicators for how programs can be improved.

PSYCHOLOGICAL TESTS

Psychological tests are designed to measure individual characteristics. The test may be administered to an individual or to a group. Their purpose is to measure abilities, achievements, aptitudes, interests, attitudes, values, and personality characteristics. The results can be used to plan instruction, to study differences between individuals and groups, and for counseling and guidance.

Ability refers to the current level of knowledge or skill in a particular area. Three types of psychological tests—**intelligence tests, achievement tests,** and **aptitude tests**—are categorized as ability tests because they measure facets of ability. Young children are often measured to determine the progress of their development. A measure used with such children may assess ability in motor, language, social, or cognitive skills. The *McCarthy Scales of Children's Abilities* (McCarthy, 1972), for example, has indices for verbal, perceptual/performance, quantitative, cognitive, memory, and motor abilities.

Achievement is related to the extent to which a person has acquired certain information or mastered identified skills. An achievement test measures ability in that it evaluates the child's achievement related to specific prior instruction. The *Peabody Individual Achievement Test* (Dunn & Markwardt, 1970) is a measure of achievement in mathematics, reading recognition, reading comprehension, spelling, and general information.

Aptitude is the potential to learn or develop proficiency in some area, provided that certain conditions or training are available. An individual may have a high aptitude for music or art. Like achievement tests, aptitude tests also measure learned abilities. An aptitude test measures the results of both general and incidental learning and predicts future learning.

Intelligence tests are ability tests in that they assess overall intellectual functioning. They are also aptitude tests because they assess aptitude for learning and problem solving. The *Stanford-Binet Scale* (Terman & Merrill, 1973) is an example of an intelligence scale that also measures individual aptitude.

Personality tests measure the person's tendency to behave in a particular way. Such tests are used to diagnose children's emotional problems. Because an inventory is used to assess personality characteristics, the test is quite lengthy, usually containing several hundred items in a true-false format. Test items are answered by the parent or child or by both together, and are analyzed to determine whether the child has certain personality traits.

Interest inventories are used to determine a person's interest in a certain area or vocation and are not used with very young children. A school-age child may be given a reading interest inventory to provide the teacher with information that will serve as a guide when helping the child select reading material.

Attitudes are also measured in older children and adults, rather than in young children. An **attitude measure** determines how a person is predisposed to think about or behave toward an object, event, institution, type of behavior, or person or group of people. Politicians frequently use such measures to determine the attitudes of voters on controversial issues.

Tests for Infants

Various psychological tests have been constructed for infants and young children. Such testing is challenging because of the child's developmental limitations. Babies are particularly difficult to evaluate because of their short attention span. Their periods of alertness are brief, and they have their own schedules of opportune moments for testing. In addition, developmental changes occur rapidly, making test results unreliable for more than a short time. Generally, because of these limitations, the validity and reliability of infant scales are questionable. The tests are difficult to administer and interpret. Nevertheless, they are useful in evaluating the status of newborns and infants (Wodrich, 1984).

The status of the newborn baby can be determined by various measures. The *Apgar Scale,* administered 1 minute and 5 minutes after birth, assesses the health of the newborn by evaluating the heart rate, respiratory effort, muscle tone, body color, and reflex irritability. Each characteristic is scored on a scale of 0 to 2. A score of 7 to 10 indicates the infant is in good condition, while a score of 5 may indicate developmental difficulties. A score of 3 or below is very serious and indicates an emergency concerning the infant's survival (Santrock, 1988). The *Brazelton Neonatal Behavior Scale,* another neonatal measure (Als, Tronick, Lester, & Brazelton, 1979), measures temperamental differences, nervous system functions, and the capacity of the neonate to interact. Its purpose is to locate mild neurological dysfunctions and variations in temperament.

Infant development scales go beyond measuring neonatal status to focus on development from 1 month to 2 years. The *Gesell Developmental Schedules* (Yang, 1979) were the first scales devised to measure infant development. Gesell designed them to detect infants who were delayed in development and might need special services. The *Bayley Scales of Infant Development* (Bayley, 1933) were designed to learn about the infant's intelligence rather than overall development. While the Gesell and Bayley instruments are difficult and tedious to administer because of their length, the *Denver Developmental Screening Test* (Frankenburg, Dodds, Fandal, Kazuk, & Cohrs, 1975) is a simple instrument designed to identify children who are likely to have significant delays and need early identification and intervention. Figure 2.1 gives information about some neonatal and infant tests, and Figure 2.2 provides examples of items on the revised form of this test.

Tests for Preschool Children

Psychologists have designed a variety of tests to evaluate development and developmental problems during the preschool years. Just as testing infants and toddlers presents challenges to test administrators because of their developmental limitations, evaluations of preschool children under 6 years of age must also be conducted with their developmental characteristics in mind. With knowledge of how preschool children best respond to evaluation tasks, instruments that assess characteristics used to identify developmental delays or diagnose sources of handicaps that put the young child at risk for learning are administered to one child

Name	Level	Type	Purpose
Apgar Scale	Neonate	Birth status	Assess health of the newborn infant
Brazelton Neonatal Assessment Scale	Neonate	Neonatal status	Locate mild neurological dysfunctions and variations in temperament
Bayley Scales of Infant Development	Infant	Intelligence	Diagnose developmental delays in infants
Gesell Developmental Schedules	Infant	Developmental	Detect developmental delays
Denver Developmental Screening Test-Revised	1 month to 6 years	Developmental screening	Identify significant developmental delays

FIGURE 2.1
Neonatal and infant tests

at a time. Test items are concrete tasks or activities that match the child's ability to respond; nevertheless, validity and reliability are affected by such factors as the child's limited attention span and willingness to attempt to respond to the examiner.

Preschool intelligence tests and adaptive behavior scales are used to diagnose mental retardation. Although intelligence measures during the preschool years are generally unreliable because children's IQ can change enormously between early childhood and adolescence, they are used with young children to measure learning potential.

The *Stanford-Binet Intelligence Scale* (Terman & Merrill, 1973), the original IQ test, was designed to assess general thinking or problem-solving ability. It is valuable in answering questions about developmental delay and retardation. Conversely, the *McCarthy Scales of Children's Abilities* (McCarthy, 1972) is useful in identifying mild retardation and learning disabilities. Another instrument, the *Wechsler Preschool and Primary Scale of Intelligence* (Wechsler, 1967), is used to identify signs of uneven development.

Measures of adaptive behavior assess possible developmental problems related to learning disabilities. Adaptive behavior instruments attempt to measure how well the young child has mastered everyday living tasks such as toileting, feeding, and other skills.

The *Vineland Social Maturity Scale* (Doll, 1965) assesses the everyday behavior of the child that indicates the level of development. The *Developmental Indicators for the Assessment of Learning-Revised (DIAL-R)* (Mardel-Czundowski & Goldenberg, 1983) can be used to screen a child for overall developmental delay, and the *AAMD*

DATE

NAME

DIRECTIONS   BIRTHDATE

HOSP. NO.

1. Try to get child to smile by smiling, talking or waving to him. Do not touch him.
2. When child is playing with toy, pull it away from him. Pass if he resists.
3. Child does not have to be able to tie shoes or button in the back.
4. Move yarn slowly in an arc from one side to the other, about 6" above child's face.
   Pass if eyes follow 90° to midline. (Past midline; 180°)
5. Pass if child grasps rattle when it is touched to the backs or tips of fingers.
6. Pass if child continues to look where yarn disappeared or tries to see where it went. Yarn
   should be dropped quickly from sight from tester's hand without arm movement.
7. Pass if child picks up raisin with any part of thumb and a finger.
8. Pass if child picks up raisin with the ends of thumb and index finger using an over hand
   approach.

9. Pass any en-   10. Which line is longer?   11. Pass any   12. Have child copy
    closed form.   (Not bigger.) Turn   crossing   first. If failed,
    Fail continuous   paper upside down and   lines.   demonstrate
    round motions.   repeat. (3/3 or 5/6)

    When giving items 9, 11 and 12, do not name the forms. Do not demonstrate 9 and 11.

13. When scoring, each pair (2 arms, 2 legs, etc.) counts as one part.
14. Point to picture and have child name it. (No credit is given for sounds only.)

FIGURE 2.2
Denver Developmental Screening Test: examples of test items.
Source: Frankenburg et al., 1975.

(American Association on Mental Deficiency) *Adaptive Behavior Scale* (Lambert, 1984) assesses adaptive behavior, but in addition measures other categories, such as language development and socialization. Figure 2.3 provides a sample of behaviors assessed with the *AAMD Adaptive Behavior Scale*. Figure 2.4 presents the characteristics of preschool tests.

Tests for School-Age Children

When the child is old enough to attend preschool and elementary school, many tests are available for use by teachers, school psychologists, program evaluators, and other personnel with responsibilities for students and the early childhood curriculum. In addition to preschool programs for handicapped children, many states conduct programs for 4-year-old and kindergarten children as well. Although individual tests are available for some purposes in these programs, group testing is also used. Group tests require the child to use paper and pencil; therefore, test results may be affected by the child's ability to respond in this

DOMAIN 1
Independent Functioning

Ⓐ Eating Subdomain

ITEM 1   **Use of Table Utensils**
(Circle only one)

Uses knife and fork correctly and neatly	6
Uses table knife for cutting and spreading	5
Feeds self with spoon and fork, neatly	4
Feeds self with spoon and fork, considerable spilling	3
Feeds self with spoon, neatly	2
Feeds self with spoon, considerable spilling	1
Feeds self with fingers, or must be fed	0

ITEM 2   **Eating in Public**
(Circle only one)

Orders complete meals in restaurants	3
Orders simple meals like hamburgers and hot dogs	2
Orders soft drinks at soda fountains or canteens	1
Does not order at public eating places	0

ITEM 3   **Drinking**
(Circle only one)

Drinks without spilling, holding glass in one hand	3
Drinks from cup or glass unassisted, neatly	2
Drinks from cup or glass unassisted, considerable spilling	1
Does not drink from cup or glass unassisted	0

ITEM 4   **Table Manners**
(Circle all that apply)

Swallows food without chewing	1
Chews food with mouth open	1
Drops food on table or floor	1
Uses napkin incorrectly or not at all	1
Talks with mouth full	1
Takes food off others' plates	1
Eats too fast or too slow	1
Plays in food with fingers	1
Has no problem with the above	0
Does not demonstrate the above, e.g., because he or she is bedfast or has liquid food only	8

Ⓐ SUBDOMAIN TOTAL (Add Items 1–4)

FIGURE 2.3
AAMD Adaptive Behavior Scale: examples of behaviors.
Source: Lambert, 1984.

manner. Test validity and reliability may be affected by the child's ability both to respond in a group setting and to use a pencil to find and mark responses on the test. As students move into the primary grades, these factors become less important.

Many preschool programs are designed for children who are at high risk for learning disabilities. There are bilingual programs for children whose first language is not English, intervention programs for children who have a physical or mental handicap, and preschool programs for children from low-income homes who lack the early childhood experiences that predict successful learning. These programs may use a screening instrument to determine which children are eli-

Name	Level	Type	Purpose
Stanford-Binet Intelligence Scale	Ages 2–adult	Global intelligence	To detect delays and mental retardation
McCarthy Scales of Children's Abilities	Ages 2½–8	Intelligence	To identify and diagnose delays in cognitive and noncognitive areas through subtests
Wechsler Preschool and Primary Scale of Intelligence	Ages 4–6	Intelligence	To identify signs of uneven development; to detect overall delay
Vineland Social Maturity Scale	Ages 1–25	Adaptive behavior	To assess if the child has mastered living skills expected for the age level in terms of everyday behavior
AAMD Adaptive Behavior Scale	Ages 3–16	Adaptive behavior	Assesses adaptive behavior in terms of personal independence and development; can be compared to norms for children in regular, mildly retarded, and severely retarded classes
Developmental Indicators for the Assessment of Learning	Ages 2–5	Developmental	Assesses motor, language, and cognitive development

FIGURE 2.4
Preschool Tests

gible. Thus the *Bilingual Syntax Measure* (Burt, Dulay, & Hernandez, 1976) is a standardized test that can be used to screen children for language ability and dominance, and the *Wechsler Intelligence Scale for Children-Revised (WISC-R)* (Wechsler, 1974) and the *Bender Gestalt Test* (Bender, 1946) may be administered to a preschool or school-age, handicapped child by a **school psychologist** or **school diagnostician** to determine if the child needs educational services in a program for early childhood, handicapped children. Poor performance on the Bender Test by a school-age child indicates the need for further study of the child (Cronbach, 1984). The *Peabody Picture Vocabulary Test-Revised* (Dunn & Dunn, 1981) provides information on a child's language ability that can help determine if a child will benefit from a language enrichment program.

Achievement tests are useful when making decisions about instruction. If a child is exhibiting learning difficulties, a psychologist might administer the *Peabody Individual Achievement Test* (Dunn & Markwardt, 1970) or the *Wide Range Achievement Test* (Jastak & Jastak, 1978) to gain information about specific learning disabilities. The *Early School Inventory* (Nurss & McGauvran, 1976) or the *Boehm Test of Basic Concepts* (Boehm, 1971) might be administered by the teacher to young children to determine their need for instruction in basic concepts or to assess successful learning of concepts previously taught.

Primary-grade teachers also may need specific information about a child who is having difficulties in the classroom. Diagnostic tests such as the *Brigance Diagnostic Inventory of Basic Skills* (Brigance, 1976) or the *Diagnostic Reading Scales* (Spache, 1981) can be administered by classroom teachers to pinpoint skills in which students need additional instruction. Figure 2.5 shows information for assessing common signs on the *Brigance Diagnostic Inventory of Early Development* (Brigance, 1978). Figure 2.6 presents information about tests used with school-age children.

Group achievement tests are used to evaluate individual achievement, group achievement, and program effectivness. A school district may administer achievement tests every year to determine each student's progress, as well as to gain diagnostic information on the child's need for future instruction. The same test results can be used at the district level to give information on student progress between and within schools and to determine the effectiveness of the district's instructional program.

Instructional effectiveness may also be evaluated at the state or national level. A state agency may administer statewide achievement tests to work toward establishing a standard of instructional effectiveness in all schools within the state. Test results can identify school districts that both exceed and fall below the set standard. Indicators of poor instructional areas in many school districts will pinpoint weaknesses in the state's instructional program and facilitate specific types of improvement. National assessments are made periodically to pinpoint strengths and weaknesses in the educational progress of American children in different subject areas. These findings are frequently compared with achievement results of students in other countries.

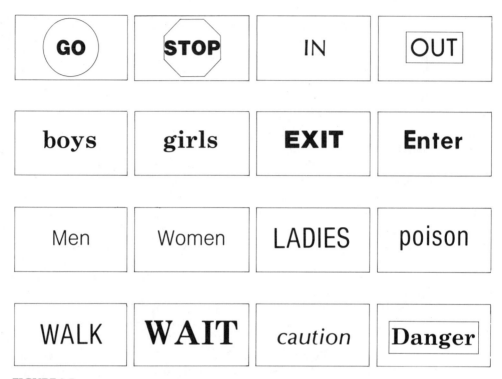

FIGURE 2.5
Brigance Diagnostic Inventory of Early Development: examples of assessment tasks
Source: BRIGANCE® *Diagnostic Inventory of Early Development,* Copyright © 1978 Curriculum Associates, Inc. Reprinted by permission. BRIGANCE® is a registered trademark of Curriculum Associates, Inc.

INFORMAL EVALUATION STRATEGIES

Standardized tests are not the only tools available for evaluation and assessment. There are various types of informal instruments and strategies to determine development and learning.

School districts often use informal tests or evaluation strategies developed by local teachers or staff members. In early childhood programs, an informal screening test may be administered to preschool children at registration to determine their instructional needs. Likewise, the speech teacher may use a simple screening instrument to evaluate the child's language development or possible speech difficulties.

Observation

One of the most valuable ways to become aware of the individual characteristics of young children is through observation. Developmental indicators in early childhood are more likely to be noted from children's behavior in natural circumstances than from a designed evaluation or instrument. Adults who observe children as

READS COMMON SIGNS

SKILL: Reads common signs:	5-3GO	STOP	IN	OUT	
BOYS	GIRLS	EXIT	ENTER	6-3MEN	
WOMEN	LADIES	POISON	WALK	WAIT	
CAUTION	DANGER7-0				

DEVELOPMENTAL RECORD BOOK: Page 20

ASSESSMENT METHOD: Child's performance

MATERIALS: Page C-206

DISCONTINUE: After 3 consecutive failures

TIME: No limit

ACCURACY: Give credit for each correct response

DEVELOPMENTAL AGE: The developmental ages are based on the performance of the child entering kindergarten with a mean age of 5 years 3 months, and often learning half of the words in kindergarten and the other half in first grade.

DIRECTIONS: Point to the "Common Signs" on page C-206 and

Say: These are words we often see on signs. Look at each word carefully and say it aloud. Begin here (point to the word "GO").

When the child responds, point to the following words, one at a time and going across the page.

After the first error (or word which the child cannot read),

Ask: Can you find any other signs on this page you can read?

Allow time for the child to look at the other words. Give encouragement if needed.

NOTES:

a. **Alternate Method of Assessment:** Reproduce and cut a copy of the child page so the words can be presented individually..

b. **Assessing for Comprehension:** You may wish to assess the child's comprehension and only give credit in the *Developmental Record Book* when the child provides an explanation indicating understanding. Ask questions such as:

• **What does this sign mean?**

• **Where do we see it?**

• **What do we do when we see this sign?**

c. **Correlation with the** *Inventory of Basic Skills:* A more comprehensive list of words and phrases frequently seen on common signs can be found in Test A-6 of the *Inventory of Basic Skills.*

d. **Additional Relevant Words:** Identify any common signs which are or should be of importance to the child, and add them to the list on the child page.

e. **Resource Materials:** Two instructional aids for teaching common signs, each of which includes over 40 common signs, are:

• *Signs & Symbols Flash Cards*—Milton Bradley Co.
Cat. # MB 7583
• *Functional Signs*—Developmental Learning Materials
Cat. # 190

OBJECTIVE: By _____(date)_____, when presented with a list of 16 words frequently seen on signs, __(child's name)__ will correctly pronounce ___(quantity)___ of them.

FIGURE 2.5
(continued)

they play and work in individual or group activities are able to determine progress in all categories of development. The child who shows evidence of emerging prosocial skills by playing successfully in the playground is demonstrating significant growth in social development. Children who struggle to balance materials on both sides of a balance beam demonstrate visible signs of cognitive growth. Physical development can be evaluated by observing children using playground equipment. Because young children learn best through active involvement with their environment, evaluation of learning may be assessed most appropriately by observing the child during periods of activity. Observation records can be used to plan instruction, to report progress in various areas of development, and to keep track of progress in mastery of preschool curriculum objectives.

Teacher-Designed Measures

Teachers have always used tests that they have devised to measure the level of learning after instruction. Early childhood teachers are more likely to use concrete tasks or oral questions for informal assessment with young children. Teachers frequently incorporate evaluation with instruction or learning experiences. Activ-

Name	Level	Type	Purpose
Bilingual Syntax Measure	Kindergarten–Grade 2	Language	To determine language dominance
Wechsler Intelligence Scale for Children Revised	Ages 6½–16½	Intelligence	To diagnose mental retardation and learning disability; includes verbal and performance subscales
Bender Gestalt Test	Ages 4–10	Visual motor functioning	To assess perceptual skills and hand–eye coordination, identifying learning disabilities
Peabody Picture Vocabulary Test Revised	Ages 2½–18	Vocabulary	To measure receptive vocabulary for standard American English
Peabody Individual Achievement Test	Kindergarten–Grade 12	Individual achievement	To assess achievement in mathematics, reading, spelling, and general information
Metropolitan Early School Inventory	Kindergarten	Developmental	To assess physical, cognitive, language, and social-emotional development
Boehm Test of Basic Concepts	Kindergarten–Grade 2	Cognitive ability	To screen for beginning school concepts
Brigance Diagnostic Inventory of Basic Skills	Kindergarten–Grade 6	Academic achievement	To assess academic skills and diagnose learning difficulties in language, math, and reading
Spache Diagnostic Reading Scales	Grade 1–8 reading levels	Diagnostic reading test	To locate reading problems and plan remedial instruction

FIGURE 2.6
School-age tests

ities and games can be used both to teach and to evaluate what the child has learned. Evaluation can also be conducted through learning centers or as part of a teacher-directed lesson. Although pencil-and-paper tests are also a teacher-designed measure, they should not be used until children are comfortable with writing.

Checklists

Developmental checklists or other forms of learning objective sequences are used at all levels of preschool, elementary, and secondary schools. Often referred to as a **scope** or **sequence of skills,** a checklist is a list of the learning objectives established for areas of learning and development at a particular age, grade level, or content area.

Skills continuua are available from many sources. The teacher may construct one, or a school district may distribute checklists for each grade level. Educational textbook publishers frequently include a skills continuum for teachers to use as an instructional guide with the textbook they have selected. State education agencies now publish objectives to be used by all school districts in the state. For example, the Texas Education Agency has distributed comprehensive skills continua commonly referred to as *Essential Elements* (Texas Education Agency, 1985) for every grade level and subject area taught in the public schools. The *Essential Elements* serve as an educational framework to assure that all school districts in Texas adhere to certain instructional goals and objectives in the curriculum.

SUMMARY

There are many reasons that we need to be able to evaluate the growth and development of young children. Specialists who work with children from various perspectives have devised formal and informal measures that can be used with newborn infants, as well as later in the early childhood years. Members of the medical profession, psychologists, educators and parents all have interest and concern for knowing that the young child is developing at a normal rate. If development deviates from acceptable progress in some way, tests and other evaluation strategies are available to study the child and devise early intervention measures that can minimize or eliminate the developmental problem.

Summary Statements

1. Infants and young children are measured and evaluated to assess their health and development and to identify developmental delays or handicaps.
2. Formal and informal methods used to measure and evaluate infants and young children include medical examinations, observation of behaviors, and psychological tests and nonstandardized instruments.

3. Evaluations are done to measure normal development and to detect advanced or delayed development.
4. Psychological tests are designed to measure intelligence, achievement, and aptitude.
5. Tests for infants include neonatal and infant development scales.
6. Preschool intelligence tests and adaptive behavior scales are used to diagnose mental retardation.
7. Tests for school-age children are used to identify children who are at risk for learning disabilities, to evaluate achievement, and to gather diagnostic information about learning needs and instructional effectiveness.
8. Informal evaluation instruments and strategies are used to measure development, to assess learning, and to plan instruction.

REVIEW QUESTIONS

1. Describe several purposes for measuring and evaluating infants and young children.
2. Who are the professionals who test young children?
3. How can a young child's development be atypical? Give examples.
4. What are the differences between achievement tests, aptitude tests, and intelligence tests? Give examples.
5. Why are infant neonatal scales administered? Infant development scales?
6. What is the purpose of preschool intelligence tests? How are adaptive scales used? Give examples.
7. Why do schools administer tests to preschool children? Describe the purposes.
8. Name preschool tests that teachers can administer and tests that school psychologists must administer.
9. How do schools use group achievement tests? State education agencies? National agencies?
10. How are informal measures different from psychological or standardized tests?
11. Why is observation an important evaluation method to use with young children?

KEY TERMS

achievement test   attitude measure

aptitude test   developmental checklist informal tests

intelligence test

interest inventory

learning disability

neonatologist

obstetrician

pediatrician

personality test

psychological test

school diagnostician

school psychologist

scope (sequence of skills)

standardized test

REFERENCES

Als, H., Tronick, E., Lester, B. M., & Brazelton, T. B. (1979). Specific neonatal measures: The Brazelton neonatal behavioral assessment scale. In J. D. Osofsky (Ed.), *Handbook of infant development*. New York: Wiley.

Apgar, V. (1975). A proposal for a new method of evaluation of a newborn infant. *Anesthesia and Analgesia, 32*, 260–267.

Bayley, N. (1933). *The California First-Year Mental Scale*. Berkeley: University of California Press.

Bender, L. (1946). *Bender Gestalt Test: Cards and manual of instructions*. New York: American Orthopsychiatric Association.

Boehm, A. (1971). *Boehm Test of Basic Concepts: Manual*. New York: Psychological Corp.

Brigance, A. H. (1976). *Brigance Diagnostic Inventory of Basic Skills*. Woburn, MA: Curriculum Associates.

Brigance, A. H. (1978). *Brigance Diagnostic Inventory of Early Development*. Woburn, MA: Curriculum Associates.

Burt, M. K., Dulay, H. C., & Hernandes, E. C. (1976). *Bilingual Syntax Measure*. New York: Harcourt Brace Jovanovich.

Cronbach, L. J. (1984). *Essentials of psychological testing*. New York: Harper & Row.

Doll, E. A. (1965). *Vineland Social Maturity Scale: Condensed manual of directions*. Circle Pines, MN: American Guidance Service.

Dunn, L. M., & Dunn, L. (1981). *Peabody Picture Vocabulary Test-Revised*. Circle Pines, MN: American Guidance Service.

Dunn, L. M., & Markwardt, F. C. (1970). *Peabody Individual Achievement Test*. Circle Pines, MN: American Guidance Service.

Frankenburg, W. K., Dodds, J. B., Fandal, A. W., Kazuk, E., & Cohrs, M. (1975). *Denver Developmental Screening Test: Reference manual*. Denver: University of Colorado Medical Center.

Jastak, J. F., & Jastak, S. (1978). *The Wide Range Achievement Test: Manual of instructions*. Wilmington, DE: Jastak Associates.

Lambert, N. (1984). *Diagnostic and technical manual: AAMD Adaptive Behavior Scale, School Edition*. Monterey, CA: CTB/McGraw-Hill.

Mardell-Czundowski, C. D., & Goldenberg, D. S. (1983). *Developmental Indicators for the Assessment of Learning-Revised (DIAL-R)*. Edison, NJ: Childcraft Education Corp.

McCarthy, D. (1972). *Manual for the McCarthy Scales of Children's Abilities*. New York: Psychological Corp.

Nurss, J. R., & McGauvran, M. E. (1976). *Early School Inventory*. New York: Harcourt Brace Jovanovich.

Santrock, J. W. (1988). *Children*. Dubuque, IA: Wm. C. Brown.

Sattler, J. M. (1982). *Assessment of Children's Intelligence and Special Abilities* (2nd ed.). Boston: Allyn and Bacon.

Spache, G. D. (1981). *Diagnostic Reading Scales: Examiner's manual*. Monterey, CA: CTB/McGraw-Hill.

Texas Education Agency. (1985). *State Board of Education rules for curriculum. Principles, standards, and procedures for accreditation of school districts*. Austin: Author.

Terman, L. M., & Merrill, M. A. (1973). *Stanford-Binet Intelligence Scale: Manual for the third revision Form L–M*. Boston: Houghton Mifflin.

Wechsler, D. (1967). *Wechsler Preschool and Primary Scale of Intelligence: Manual*. New York: Psychological Corp.

Wechsler, D. (1974). *Manual for the Wechsler Intelligence Scale for Children-Revised*. New York: Psychological Corp.

Wodrich, D. (1984). *Children's psychological testing*. Baltimore: Paul H. Brooks.

Yang, R. K. (1979). Early infant assessment: An overview. In J. D. Osofsky (Ed.), *Handbook of infant development*. New York: Wiley & Sons.

3

Standardized Tests

In Chapter 2, various methods and purposes for measuring and evaluating infants and young children were discussed. We differentiated between formal measures and informal methods of measurement. Psychological tests and some educational tests are considered formal instruments because they have been standardized.

How are standardized tests different from other kinds of measures? What are their advantages? In this chapter, we discuss how standardized tests are designed and tried out to measure the desired characteristics. Test validity and reliability will be explained, as well as their effect on the dependability of the test.

People who use standardized tests with young children must be able to interpret the results. To understand more clearly how scores on a test are translated into meaningful information, raw scores and standard scores will be described. The normal curve and its role in interpreting test scores will also be explained.

STEPS IN STANDARDIZED TEST DESIGN

Test designers follow a series of steps when constructing a new test. These steps ensure that the test achieves its goals and purposes. In planning a test, the

developers first decide what its purpose will be. Next, the test format is determined. As actual test design begins, objectives are formulated; test items are
written, tried out, and analyzed; and the final test form is assembled. When the
final test form is administered, norms can be established and the validity and
reliability of the test can be determined. The final step is to develop a test manual
containing procedures for administering the test and statistical information on
standardization results.

Specifying the Purpose of the Test

Every standardized test should have a clearly defined purpose. The description
of the test's purpose is the framework for the construction of the test. It also
allows evaluation of the instrument when design and construction steps are
completed. The *Standards for Educational and Psychological Tests and Manuals* (American Psychological Association, 1974) has established the standards for including
the test's purpose in the test manual. They are as follows:

> B2. The test manual should state explicitly the purpose and applications for which
> the test is recommended. (p. 14)
> B3. The test manual should describe clearly the psychological, educational and
> other reasoning underlying the test and the nature of the characteristic it is in-
> tended to measure. (p. 15)

Test designers should be able to explain what construct or characteristics the test
will measure, how the test results will be used, and who will take the test or to
whom it will be administered.

The population for whom the test is intended is a major factor in test design.
Tests constructed for infants and young children are very different from tests
designed for adults. As test developers consider the composition and characteristics of the children for whom they are designing the test, they must include
variables such as age, intellectual or educational level, socioeconomic background,
cultural background, and whether or not the young child is able to read.

Determining Test Format

Test format decisions are based on determinations made about the purpose of the
test and the characteristics of the test takers. The test format results from the
developer's decision on how test items will be presented and how the test taker
will respond (Brown, 1983). One consideration is whether the test will be verbal
or written. Although adults are most familiar with written tests, infants and
young children are unable to read or write. Tests designed for very young children
usually are presented orally by a test administrator. Another alternative is to use
a psychomotor response. The child is given an object to manipulate or performs
a physical task.

For older children, high school students, and adults, other test formats are
possible. Test takers may respond to an alternative-choice written test such as
one with true–false, **multiple-choice,** or matching items. The test can be given as

PURPOSE OF AND RATIONALE FOR SELECTED TESTS

The test developers of the *K-ABC Kaufman Assessment Battery for Children* (Kaufman & Kaufman, 1983) state its purpose as follows:

> The K-ABC is intended for psychological and clinical assessment, psychoeducational evaluation of learning-disabled and other exceptional children, educational planning and placement, minority group assessment, preschool assessment, neuropsychological assessment, and research. (p. 2)

Information about the expected uses of the *Peabody Picture Vocabulary Test-Revised Manual, Forms L and M* (Dunn & Dunn, 1981) includes school, clinical, vocational, and research uses. Part of the school use description follows:

> Since the PPVT-R is a reasonably good measure of scholastic aptitude for subjects where the language of the home is Standard English, it should also be useful as an initial *screening device* in scanning for bright, low-

ability, and language impaired children who may need special attention. Too, it should be helpful in identifying underachievers, when used in conjunction with a measure of school achievement. (p. 3)

The *California Achievement Tests, Forms E and F* (1985) are described as follows:

> This latest edition of the California Achievement Tests will continue to provide the accurate measurement in the basic skills for which the CAT series has been noted. It will continue, for example, to serve well the measurement and evaluation of such programs as Chapter I, ECIA. This new, improved, and augmented test battery will also be of special value to those schools seeking an assessment system that will help them work toward, and achieve greater excellence. CAT E & F will thus meet the full range of information requirements of today's schools. (p. 4)

a **group test,** rather than being administered as an **individual test** to one person at a time. Short-answer and essay items are also a possibility.

After the test designers have selected the format most appropriate for the test's purpose and for the group to be tested, actual test construction begins. Experimental test forms are assembled after defining test objectives and writing test items for each objective.

Developing Experimental Forms

In preparing preliminary test forms, developers again use the test purpose description as their guide. Test content is now delimited. If an achievement test for school children is to be written, for example, curriculum is analyzed to ensure that the test will reflect the instructional program. If the achievement test is designed for national use, textbook series, syllabi, and curricular materials are studied to check that test objectives will accurately reflect curriculum trends. Teachers and curriculum experts will be consulted to review the content outlines and behavioral objectives that serve as reference points for test items.

The process of developing good test items involves writing, editing, trying out, and rewriting or revising test items. Before being tried out, each item for an achievement test may be reviewed and rewritten by test writers, teachers, and other experts in the field. Many more items than will be used are written, since many will be eliminated in the editing and rewrite stages (Burrill, 1980).

A preliminary test is assembled so that the selected test items can be tried out with a sample of students. The experimental test forms resemble the final form. Instructions are written for administering the test. The test may have more questions than will be used in the final form because many questions will be revised or eliminated after the tryout. The sample of people selected to take the preliminary test are similar to the population who will take the final form of the test.

The tryout of the preliminary test form is described as *item tryout and analysis*. **Item analysis** involves studying three characteristics of each test question: difficulty level, discrimination, and grade progression in difficulty. The *difficulty level* of a question refers to how many test takers in the tryout group answered the question correctly. *Discrimination* of each question involves the extent to which the question distinguishes between test takers who did well or poorly on the test. Test takers who did well should have been more successful in responding to an item than test takers who did poorly. The item differentiates between people who have greater or less knowledge or ability. The *grade progression* of difficulty refers to tests that are taken by students in different grades in school. If a test question has good grade progression of difficulty, a greater percentage of students should answer it correctly in each successively higher grade (Burrill, 1980).

Assembling the Test

After item analysis is completed, the next step is to assemble the final form of the test. As a result of item analysis, test items have been reexamined, rewritten, or eliminated. Test questions or required behaviors to measure each test objective are selected for the test. If more than one test form is to be used, developers must ensure that alternate **forms** are **equivalent** in content and difficulty. Test directions are finalized with instructions for both test takers and test administrators. In addition, information for test administrators includes details about the testing environment and testing procedures.

Standardizing the Test

Although test construction is complete when the final form is assembled and printed, the test has not yet been standardized. The final test form must be administered to another, larger sample of test takers to acquire norm data. **Norms** provide the tool whereby children's test performance can be compared with the performance of a reference group.

A reference group that represents the children for whom the test has been designed is selected to take the test for the purpose of establishing **norms.** The performance of the reference or sample group on the final test form during the standardization process will be used to evaluate the test scores of individuals and/ or groups who take the test in the future.

The norming group is chosen to reflect the makeup of the population for whom the test is designed. If a national school achievement test is being developed, the standardization sample will include children from all sections of the country to include such variables as sex, age, community size, geographic area, and socioeconomic and ethnic factors. For other types of tests, different characteristics may be used to match the norming sample with future populations to be tested.

Various kinds of norms can be established during the standardization process. Raw scores of sample test takers are converted into derived scores or standard scores for purposes of comparison. Standard scores are achieved by calculating the **raw score,** or the number of items answered correctly, into a score that can be used to establish a norm. Various types of standard scores can be used to compare the people selected to standardize the test and future populations who will be given the test. Each type of **grade norm** allows test users to interpret a child's test scores in comparison with the scores of children used to norm the test (Burrill, 1980). For example, an age score is established by determining the norms for age groups when the test is given to the norming sample. The age norms describe the average performance of children of various ages. Likewise, grade norms or grade equivalent norms are established by determining the average scores made by children at different grade levels in the norming group (Brown, 1983).

Developing the Test Manual

The final step in test design is development of the test manual. The test developer describes the purpose of the test, the development of the test, and the standardization procedures. Information on test validity and reliability is also included to give test users information on the dependability of the test. When explaining standardization information in the users' manual, test developers will describe the method used to select the norming group. The number of individuals included in standardizing the test is reported, as well as the geographic areas, types of communities, socioeconomic groups, and ethnic groups they represent.

Validity and Reliability

Norm information is important for establishing confidence in analyzing and interpreting the significance of test scores. Test users also need information demonstrating that the test will be valuable for the intended purposes; therefore, the test manual also provides information on validity and reliability. Both types of dependability indicators are equally important in determining the quality of the test. **Validity** is the degree to which the test serves the purpose for which it will be used, while **reliability** is the extent to which a test is stable or consistent. Test validity can be determined through content validity, criterion-related validity, or construct validity.

When first designing a test, the developers describe its purpose. Test objectives or the test outlines provide the framework for the content of the test. When information is provided on **content validity,** the test developers are defining the degree to which the test items measured the test objectives and fulfilled the purpose of the test. Thus, for example, on an achievement test, content validity is the extent to which the content of the test represents an adequate sampling of the instructional program it is intended to cover.

Criterion-related validity is related to the validity of an aptitude test. Rather than analyzing course content, test items focus on skills or tasks that predict future success in some area. The estimates of predictive validity are concerned with stability over time. For example, an **intelligence quotient (IQ)** test might be predictive of school achievement. Likewise, the *Scholastic Aptitude Test* scores may predict whether high school students will be successful in college. Validity is predictive because the criteria for success are the future grades the student will earn in college or the student's future grade point average.

Criterion-related validity may be **concurrent** rather than predictive. Instead of using a future measure to determine validity, current measures are used. The outside criterion is assessed when the test is standardized. The developer of an intelligence test may cite an existing intelligence test as the criterion to measure validity. The author administers both intelligence tests to the sample group. If the new test scores correlate highly with scores on the existing test, they may be used to establish concurrent validity.

If a test measures an abstract psychological trait, the users' manual will describe how the sample group was tested to establish construct validity. **Construct validity** is the extent to which a test measures a relatively abstract psychological trait such as personality, verbal ability, or mechanical aptitude. Rather than examining test items developed from test objectives, one examines construct validity by comparing test results with the variables that explain the behaviors. For example, suppose that the construct is believed to include certain behavioral characteristics, such as sociability or honesty. An instrument's construct validity can be checked by analyzing how the trait is affected by changing conditions. Alternatively, an instrument may measure level of anxiety. Its construct validity is determined by creating experiments to find what conditions affect anxiety (Gronlund, 1985).

Construct validity is necessary when measuring creativity. To have construct validity, the test designed to measure creativity has to differentiate the behavior of creative people from that of uncreative people (Mehrens and Lehmann, 1984).

The validity of a test is the extent to which the test measures what it is designed to measure. Test users, however, are also interested in a test's dependability or stability in measuring behaviors. Test developers, therefore, also establish and report on the reliability of the instrument as part of the standardization process.

Test reliability is related to test item discrimination. When test items are analyzed after the initial item tryout, they are examined for discrimination power. When the final test form is administered to a norming sample, the items are again analyzed to ensure that the instrument is fairly reliable. The whole test is analyzed, rather than individual test items. The test manual will report the test's reliability as determined using alternate-form, split-half, or test-retest reliability measures. A test's reliability coefficient describes the degree to which a test is free from error of measurement. If **alternate-form reliability** strategies are used, test authors construct two equivalent forms of the final test. Both forms are administered to the norming group within a short period. The correlation between the results on the two different forms measures the coefficient of reliability.

If a **split-half reliability** coefficient is used to establish reliability, the norming group is administered a single test, and scores on one-half of the test are correlated with scores on the other half of the test. Split-half reliability is determined from the contents of the single test. A test with split-half reliability is also considered to have **internal consistency.** That is, the items on each half of the test are positively intercorrelated in measuring the same characteristics.

Test-retest reliability is also derived from the administration of a single test form; however, in this case, the test is administered to the norming group, and then administered again after a short interval. The two sets of scores are compared to determine if they were consistent in measuring the test objectives.

Standard Error of Measurement

No matter how well designed, no test is completely free from error. Although there is a hypothetical true score, in reality it does not exist. The reliability of the test depends on how large the **standard error** of measurement is after analysis of the chosen method of determining reliability. If the reliability correlations are poor, the standard error of measurement will be large. The larger the standard error of measurement, the less reliable the test. Standard error of measurement is the estimate of the amount of variation that can be expected in test scores as a result of reliability correlations.

Several variables during standardization affect test reliability. Generally, the larger the population sample, the more reliable the test will be. Another factor is the length of the test. Longer tests are usually more reliable than shorter tests. Longer tests have more test items, resulting in a better sample of behaviors. The more items there are to measure a behavior, the better the estimate of the true score and the greater the reliability.

A third variable that can affect standard error of measurement is the range of test scores obtained from the norming group. The wider the spread of scores, the more reliably the test will be able to distinguish between them. Thus, the range of the scores demonstrates how well the test discriminates between good and poor students (Gronlund, 1985).

INTERPRETING TEST SCORES

We have mentioned before that a child's performance on a standardized test is meaningless until it can be compared with other scores in a useful way. The raw score must be translated into a score that reports how well that child's performance compared with that of other children who took the same test. In describing the standardization process, we discussed how norms are set for comparing individual or group test scores based on the scores made by a norming sample. Although several different scoring systems have been established for translating and interpreting raw scores, the bell-shaped normal curve is the graph on which the distribution of scores is arranged using some type of standard score.

The Normal Curve

The normal curve (Figure 3.1) represents the ideal **normal distribution** of test scores of groups of people, as well as the distribution of many other human characteristics. Physical and psychological traits are distributed in a bell-shaped frequency polygon, with most scores clustered toward the center of the curve. If, for example, we were to chart the heights of all the adult men in the United States, most heights would be grouped around a mean height, with fewer distributed toward very short and very tall heights.

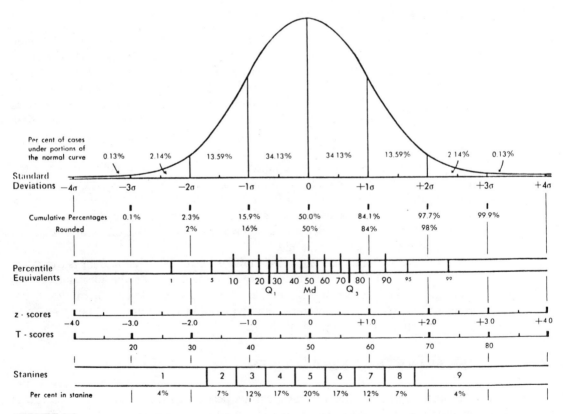

FIGURE 3.1
Normal curve

Ideally, group test scores have a similar distribution, and the normal curve can be used as a reference for understanding individual test scores. Any numerical scale can be used with the normal curve to demonstrate the range of scores on a test instrument.

The midpoint of the curve is the **mean.** Since the curve represents the total number of scores in the distribution of scores on a test, the mean divides the curve into two halves. There are as many scores distributed above the mean as below it.

The normal curve is used to describe or pinpoint an individual's perform- ance on a standardized test. Derived scores are used to specify where the indi- vidual score falls on the curve and how far above or below the mean the score falls (Cronbach, 1984).

Standard Deviations

The normal curve is further divided into eight equal sections called **standard deviations** (designated by a sigma, σ). Standard deviations are used to calculate how an individual scored compared with the scores of the norming group on a standardized test. Standard deviations describe how test scores are dispersed around the mean. For example, if the individual score was one standard deviation above the mean, this indicates that the individual scored higher than the mean of test scores on the norming sample. Further, the individual scored higher than about 84 percent of the individuals who normed the test. If we look at the percentage of scores in each standard deviation, we find that about 68 percent of the scores are found between one standard deviation below the mean and one standard deviation above the mean. The percentage of scores in each succes- sive standard deviation above and below the mean decreases sharply beyond one standard deviation. When raw scores are transformed into percentiles, or stan- dard scores, standard deviations further explain individual scores compared to the normal distribution of scores (Brown, 1983).

Percentile Ranks and Stanines

When a test is standardized, we may use percentile ranks and stanines as the measures of comparison between the norming sample and individual test scores. Figure 3.1 shows how **percentile ranks** are arrived at by looking at cumulative percentages and percentile equivalents under the normal curve. We already un- derstand that a percentage of the total distribution of scores is arranged within each standard deviation on the normal curve, with a smaller percentage located in each deviation as we move away from the mean. These percentages can also be understood in a cumulative fashion. Beginning at the negative end of the curve, percentages in each standard deviation can be added together. At the mean the cumulative percentage is 50 percent, while 99.9 percent is reached at three standard deviations above the mean.

Percentile equivalents are derived from the accumulated percentages. If the cumulative percentages represent the percentage of test scores falling into standard deviations along the normal curve, **percentiles** represent a point on the normal curve below which a percentage of test scores are distributed. A score at the 40th percentile equals or surpasses 40 percent of the scores on the test being used.

When a percentile rank norm is established for a standardized test, the developers take the distribution of scores acquired from the norming sample and determine how they are arranged on the normal curve. The distribution is calculated by standard deviations and percentiles. Future test users can then use these norms as measures of comparison to interpret individual or group scores in comparison with the scores of the original norming group.

Stanines provide another way to understand the distribution of scores. As shown in Figure 3.1, stanines divide the norm population represented by the normal scale into nine groups. Except for Stanine 9, the top, and Stanine 1, the bottom, each stanine represents one-half of a standard deviation. Stanines provide a helpful way to compare cumulative percentages and percentile ranks on the normal curve. One can look at the percentage of scores distributed in each stanine and understand how the percentile rank is correlated with the overall distribution. In reporting group test scores, the stanine rank of an individual score provides a measure of how the individual ranked within the group of test takers (Seashore, 1980).

Z Scores and T Scores

Some standardized test results are reported using Z scores or T scores. **Z scores** and **T scores** are called **standard scores** because they report how many standard deviations a person's score is located above or below the mean on the normal curve. If a person's score is one standard deviation above the mean, for example, the standard score is +1. A Z score has a zero mean, while a T score has a mean of 50 and is cumulative.

All scoring scales are drawn parallel to the baseline of the normal curve. Each uses the deviation from the mean as the reference to compare an individual score with the mean score of a group.

CONSIDERATIONS IN CHOOSING AND EVALUATING TESTS

Whenever a private school, public school district, preschool, or child care center decides to use a test to evaluate their children, one must decide how to select the best test for that purpose. Those charged with the responsibility for selecting the test have to determine the relevant questions to ask about the test. Brown (1983) identified various factors that must be considered by test users:

> the purpose of the testing, what characteristics are to be measured, how the test results will be used, the qualifications of the people who will interpret the scores and use the results, and any practical constraints. (pp. 449–450)

All of these factors are important in selecting tests for young children. Because of the developmental limitations of young test takers, test formats must be compatible with their ability to respond. Some developmental limitations include short attention span, undeveloped fine motor skills, inability to use reading skills for test responses, and poor performance on group tests. Limitations in training and experience in those who administer the test are factors in test selection.

Other relevant concerns, particularly in selecting tests for young children, are the costs involved, testing time, and ease of scoring and using test results (Cronbach, 1984). The test has to be reasonable in cost, and the time needed to administer the test should be suitable for young children.

A major issue is whether the test has quality. Is it a good test to use with the children? The person searching for an appropriate test will want to examine the test manual for indications of how well the test was designed and normed. The test manual should include information on the following:

1. The purpose of the test. The statement of purpose should include the rationale for the test, the characteristics the test is designed to measure, and the uses for the test.
2. Test design. The manual should include information on the procedures and rationale for selecting test items and on the development and trial of test forms.
3. Establishment of validity and reliability. The manual should state the procedures used to establish validity and reliability to include sufficient data on validity, reliability, and norms.
4. Test administration and scoring. The test manual should give specific information on how to administer and score the test and interpret test results. Information should be adequate for users to determine if the test is practical and suitable for their purposes. The manual should include potential problems that can be encountered when administering and scoring the test (Kaplan & Saccuzzo, 1982). See Figure 3.2 for questions that should be answered in a test manual, including an acceptable coefficient of reliability.

Test users need to have extensive training in tests and measurements to interpret a test manual adequately. For many users, the explanations and data reported in test manuals are complex and difficult to understand. The reader may have difficulty in deciding if the reliability coefficient is adequate, if the size and demographic characteristics of the norming population are appropriate, or if test content and format are suitable for the intended uses. To get additional help in understanding the suitability of the test, test users will also want to consult resources for test standards and reviews. *The Standards for Educational and Psychological Tests and Manuals* (American Psychological Association, 1974) includes standards for tests, manuals, and reports. It also includes standards for reliability and validity, as well as information that should be included on the use of tests. A less

Checklist of questions that should be answered in the test manual

Standardization Sample
1. How many subjects were used to establish the reliability, validity, and norms for the test?
2. What were the demographic and personal characteristics of these subjects? Are they similar to those of the group you will give the test to?

Reliability
1. What methods were used to estimate the reliability of the test?
2. Is the reliability high enough for your purposes (usually .90 or above for tests used to make decisions about individuals and .70 or above for research purposes)?

Validity
1. Is there evidence that the test is meaningful for *your purposes*?
2. What specific criteria was the test validated against?

Scoring
1. Are scoring keys available?
2. If the test can be scored by machine, how much does it cost and what sort of report is offered?

Practical Considerations
1. How long does it take to administer the test?
2. Does the test require reading? If so, is it at the right level for the people you will test?
3. How much training is required for the test administrator? How can the training be obtained?

FIGURE 3.2

Questions about test manuals.

Source: Kaplan and Saccuzzo, 1982.

technical resource is *Guidelines for Test Use: A Commentary on the Standards for Educational and Psychological Tests* (Brown, 1980).

There are also sources that identify, describe, and evaluate published tests. *Tests in Print II* (Buros, 1974) is a comprehensive bibliography of almost 2,500 tests. The tests are listed by type, and basic information is given about each test. The *Eighth Mental Measurement Yearbook* (Buros, 1978) includes test information and sources of information about test construction, validation, and use. Critical reviews of the tests are also included.

A resource that is particularly helpful to persons without a background in test design at a technical level is *Test Critiques, Volumes I–VII* (Keyser & Sweetland, 1984–1987). It includes information about test design and use, as well as a critique of the tests. There are other resources for test evaluation and selection that are particularly suitable for users of early childhood tests. Readers who desire more information on sourcebooks are directed to "Measuring Young Children" (Goodwin & Goodwin, 1982). Additional information on standardized tests used with young children is located in Appendix B.

Tests that have proven reliability and validity are dependable. They can be administered to many children, either individually or as a group, and children's scores can be interpreted with confidence that the results accurately reflect each child's behaviors or characteristics.

Validity, reliability, norm referencing, and other test characteristics that contribute to the effectiveness of the standardized test result from careful and thorough test design. Each step in test construction has the goal of producing a dependable test to measure a human characteristic accurately.

DISADVANTAGES OF STANDARDIZED TESTS

Although standardized tests are carefully designed and standardized before they are used with children, they are not necessarily the best method of evaluating young children. Standardized tests also have weaknesses, and many educators have concerns about the schools' increasing reliance on their results. There are also specific issues about the use of standardized tests with young children, which focus on validity and reliability, difficulties in administering standardized tests to preschool and primary school-age children, inappropriate use of test results, and the need to improve standardized tests.

Concerns About the Increased Use of Standardized Tests

Use of standardized testing in public education has increased in recent years. The movement for educational reform combined with concern about accountability has resulted in massive spending for test development and implementation. State education agencies have mandated the use of state-level achievement tests for elementary and secondary schools to compare achievement among school districts. Some states are using minimum-competency tests for high school graduation and admission to teacher education programs.

Ironically, standardized tests are increasingly being challenged at this time. Efforts to reexamine their use began in the late 1970s and continued in the 1980s. In 1972 the National Education Association (NEA) proposed a national moratorium on standardized testing, including intelligence, achievement, and aptitude tests (National Education Association, 1972). In 1977 the NEA issued a report after studying standardized tests. Although the report stated that some testing was necessary and that some measures had reliability and validity, it was critical of test content, types of test items, and specific tests (National Education Association, 1977).

Other organizations expressed similar concerns (National School Boards Association, 1977; Oakland & Laosa, 1977). The Council for Basic Education (Weber, 1977) expressed concern about several types of standardized tests used in public schools, including group IQ tests, reading readiness tests, achievement tests, and college admission tests.

The Association for Childhood Education International and the National Association of Elementary School Principals (Perrone, 1976–1978) issued a position paper questioning the usefulness and accuracy of standardized tests with children. A particular concern was the use of test results to place children in special education or remedial programs. The high proportion of children from low socioeconomic and minority populations who were placed in special education or lower-track programs was thought to be closely related to test results.

More recently, criticism has focused on government-mandated standardized testing in the schools and its impact on teachers and students. Educators have expressed doubts about the usefulness of the increase in testing (Perrone, 1981) and have deplored the control that testing has imposed on instruction (Durkin, 1987). Calfee (1987) stated that government mandated tests now dictate the curriculum in elementary schools. Labeled by some as *measurement-driven instruction*, such testing is both touted as a cost-effective way of improving the quality of public education (Popham, 1987) and criticized as reducing education to learning bits of information (Bracey, 1987).

Limitations of Standardized Tests

The report *Uses and Abuses of Standardized Testing in the Schools*, by the Council for Basic Education (Weber, 1977), described weaknesses and limitations of standardized tests. The limitations included limited test content, inaccuracy of norms such as **grade equivalent scores,** and inappropriate use of test results. Many achievement tests stressed reading and mathematics skills and gave little or no emphasis to other subjects taught in elementary schools. A fundamental weakness was that the achievement tests failed to measure important outcomes such as interest in learning, initiative, self-discipline, and skills in the arts. Two important skills, writing and speaking, were also excluded from the tests. Because test results may be used for promotion, class assignment, and assignment to special programs such as gifted or special education programs, Weber doubted that the tests were more accurate than teacher assessments.

Norm scores were also considered inadequate. Weber pointed out that a student's grade equivalent scores could vary from test to test. In addition, on some tests, the grade equivalent score could vary by as much as a year as a result of the answers to a few questions.

Despite these concerns about standardized tests, the long-term campaign to reduce their use failed. Educational reforms responding to calls for excellence in education have resulted in increased reliance on standardized testing (National Association for the Education of Young Children, 1988). As school districts are pressured by state agencies to improve students' achievement, administrators, in turn, raise their expectations of teachers in individual schools that are reflected in achievement test scores at the end of the school year. Teachers then put pressure on their students in preparing them to do well on the test. Overuse of testing and excessive reliance on test results have caused renewed concern about the limitations of standardized tests.

Group test scores can be misleading because it is difficult to ensure that achievement tests are administered correctly by classroom teachers. Because teachers or educational programs are frequently evaluated on the basis of achievement test results, coaching or other forms of assistance can occur. As a result, group test scores should be analyzed with some skepticism.

Another limitation of group scores on achievement tests is related to variables outside school instruction, including socioeconomic conditions and how much money a school district can commit for instruction. These and other factors can affect group scores regardless of the quality of instruction.

An additional criticism of standardized tests is the presence of cultural bias. These tests have been studied to determine if test items discriminate against any minority group. Although test developers have worked diligently in recent years to eliminate cultural bias, it is still a concern because all students have not had an equal opportunity to acquire the skills and knowledge being tested in many standardized tests. Guilmet (1983) found such a bias in comparing scores on a standardized preschool test between Navajo children and day care children in Los Angeles. The Navajo children had lower scores, particularly the youngest ones who lived in the least acculturated households. Guilmet concluded that testing all children with the same instrument, regardless of the cultural background, is misleading when assessing and understanding the abilities of individual children.

Test designers have found it impossible to develop a culture-free test. Instead they have tried to develop test items that do not favor specific geographical regions and to use vocabulary that is not offensive to a cultural group or favors specific groups. They also try not to use pictures or language that over- or underrepresent or stereotype a sex group. Test forms are examined for ethnic bias or selection bias that would favor some group in predicting success on a test such as a reading readiness test.

Another limitation of standardized achievement tests is the difference between the purpose of the tests and how teachers actually use test results. Salmon-Cox (1981) analyzed the usefulness of standardized achievement test scores to classroom teachers. Salmon-Cox found that although tests are thought to determine curriculum, teachers actually use their own judgment or interaction and observation skills to assess student performance or skill levels. Durkin (1987) reported that although the *Stanford Early Achievement Test* (Madden & Gardner, 1969, 1971) should have been used to assess student progress, teachers and administrators had a different perception of their purpose. They believed that the tests were to provide information for the child's permanent folder or to select children for a transitional class.

Because standardized tests take years to develop and norm, there is currently a discrepancy between what is measured on the tests and current theory about how children learn. One such mismatch is in the area of mathematics. Whereas current theory about how children learn mathematics in the primary grades stresses a Piagetian approach to acquisition of concepts about numbers, tests reflect outdated instructional methods. Current theory advocates the child's construction of concepts through active interaction with materials, whereas achievement tests measure knowledge of numerals (Kamii, 1985a, 1985b).

Current theory in reading instruction stresses a whole-language or emergent literacy approach. Current methods use the child's initiative and developmental progress in an integrated approach that includes oral language, writing, reading, and comprehension. Standardized tests, by contrast, measure more traditional reading instruction that emphasizes phonics, word recognition, and isolated skill acquisition (Farr & Carey, 1986; Teale, 1988; Teale, Hiebert, & Chittenden, 1987; Valencia & Pearson, 1987).

ISSUES IN USING STANDARDIZED TEST RESULTS WITH YOUNG CHILDREN

Many persons have serious doubts about the use of standardized tests with preschool and elementary school children. Early childhood educators and specialists are divided in their position on the use of this type of evaluation. Some are opposed to any use of standardized tests with young children. Others state that there is a place for the information they provide, particularly if the test can be improved.

Concerns About Validity and Reliability

The younger the child, the more difficult it is to develop valid and reliable instruments for measurement. Early childhood educators are cautious in using standardized tests with young children because accuracy is important if developmentally appropriate planning is to follow. In the Position Statement on Developmentally Appropriate Practice in Early Childhood Programs Serving Children from Birth Through Age 8 (National Association for the Education of Young Children, 1986), it was proposed that valid instruments for young children are extremely rare.

Cryan (1986) described difficulties with standardized tests as potentially a plague. Among other concerns, Cryan stated that test scores may result in labeling, that they are subject to error, and that norming populations can be used inappropriately when comparing children from dissimilar populations. Cryan also suggested that standardized tests are often the least appropriate measure.

The issues of validity and reliability in standardized tests developed for the early childhood years were addressed more specifically in the Position Statement on Standardized Testing of Young Children 3 Through 8 Years of Age (National Association for the Education of Young Children, 1988). Reliability and validity were declared to be difficult to obtain in standardized tests, in part because of the nature of development in young children. Due to the rapidity of developmental change and individual variations in growth and development, results from a single administration of a screening instrument must be confirmed with other periodic screening and assessment methods. Shepard and Smith (1986) proposed that

USING INAPPROPRIATE TEACHING MATERIALS AND STANDARDIZED TESTS

Mary Alice Wilson is a beginning kindergarten teacher. Although this was her first year to teach, she was not without teaching experience. Mary Alice attended college in the 1960s, taught school for 2 years, and then married. She resigned her teaching position when the first of her two children was born. To help meet college expenses for her oldest son, who will soon be graduating from high school, Mary Alice returned to a nearby university to renew her teaching credentials in preschool and elementary education. Although she felt confident about her teaching ability, she was not prepared for the changes that had taken place in the schools.

In September, Mary Alice was hired to teach a kindergarten class of children from low-income homes. To her surprise, she found that she was expected to teach first-grade academic skills with the extensive use of workbook materials. Because this practice was not compatible with her understanding of the active learning style of preschool children, Mary Alice asked why the children were required to use paper-and-pencil learning strategies. In response to Mary Alice's concerns about the use of developmentally in-appropriate practices, the principal told her that it was a response to the school district's policy to upgrade the curriculum and raise achievement standards. The principal agreed that the children were being taught inappropriately but was unable to intervene.

In October, Mary Alice was required to administer a standardized test to her students that required them to be able to mark or "bubble in" the correct answer on a multiple-choice answer sheet. Since Mary Alice knew that her students were unable to follow the instructions for performing appropriately on the test, much less to find the place to mark their answers, she and the students found the experience distressing. Mary Alice felt helpless, unable to determine what was best for the students in her classroom.

Mary Alice's frustration about what she considered to be unsound practice in teaching young children, and the stress her students were experiencing as a result of the school district's policies for instruction and testing, led her to resign in late November. She decided to work as a substitute teacher while determining whether she would be able to teach preschool children under current policies and practices.

developmental inconsistencies in 4- and 5-year-old children should result in demands for evidence of validity in early childhood tests. For example, the authors stated, no existing readiness test is sufficiently accurate to justify placing children in special programs such as transition classes. Specifically, the *Gesell School Readiness Test* (Ilg, Ames, & Gillespie, 1978) was declared to lack the standards of the American Psychological Association for validity, reliability, or normative information (Shepard & Smith, 1986).

The National Association for the Education of Young Children (NAEYC) position statement on standardized testing also addressed the issue of content validity. The test selected to measure the content of the early childhood program must be accurate. The statement proposed that not using a standardized instrument would be better than a program to fit the test. Another difficulty related to content validity was the fact that tests for young children measure only cognitive objectives. Important content areas such as social competence, self-esteem, and creativity are omitted (Katz, 1985).

Goodwin and Goodwin (1982) described how quality data should be provided in test manuals regarding validity and reliability. They stated that manuals of measures for young children are often deficient in adequate technical quality data. They also cited the cost of these tests as a deterrent to their use in large-scale testing programs involving large numbers of young children.

Difficulties in Administering Tests to Young Children

Usability is affected when standardized tests are administered to young children. The size of the test group can be a problem, as well as the length of time required for testing. Reliability is affected when young children are tested in large groups. However, more time is required when test groups are small.

There are other reasons why time is a problem when testing young children. Some instruments are lengthy, requiring young children to remain attentive beyond their developmental capacities. Evans (1974) also reported that young children in some early intervention programs were given too many tests. This criticism was echoed by Perrone (1981) in an article titled "Testing, Testing and More Testing."

The NAEYC Position Statement on Standardized Testing of Young Children 3 Through 8 Years of Age (1988) stated that young children should be tested by individuals who are not only qualified to administer the tests but are knowledgeable about the developmental needs of young children. The statement summarized the problems encountered by young children who are given standardized tests:

> Too often, standardized tests are administered to children in large groups, in unfamiliar environments, by strange people, perhaps during the first few days at a new school or under other stressful conditions. During such test administrations, children are asked to perform unfamiliar tasks, for no reason that they can understand. For test results to be valid, tests are best administered to children individually in familiar, comfortable circumstances by adults whom the child has come to know and trust and who are also qualified to administer the tests. (p. 46)

Misapplication of Test Results

A serious issue in the use of standardized tests is misapplication of test results. In question is the use of tests to keep children out of school, to place children in special education programs, to place preschool children in transitional classes that result in their spending 2 years in a pre–first grade program, or to use test results for purposes not intended by test designers.

The Council for Basic Education's report (Weber, 1977) stated that the use of standardized tests for promotion, class assignment, and placement in special programs was inappropriate. With the recent emphasis on testing to provide accountability in learning and instruction, standardized tests have been used increasingly to place preschool children. As school district boards of education and school administrators deal with the pressure to attain higher scores on achievement tests, more young children are being kept in kindergarten for an extra year or placed in transitional or "developmental" classes prior to first grade so that their test scores will be higher in the primary grades. This practice is also increasing as schools establish minimum standards for promotion.

Contrary to popular belief, retention in kindergarten, placement in a transitional first grade, or retention in first grade is not effective. Although parents and educators tend to believe that such placements are a solution for immaturity (Byrnes & Yamamoto, 1984), a review of the research on retention (Holmes & Matthews, 1984) concluded that children make progress during the year that they repeat a grade, but not as much progress as children who are promoted. Similar results were found between children who were placed in a prekindergarten or transitional first grade because they were not "ready." A review of research on such transitional placements (Gredler, 1984) determined that they are no more successful than retention in a grade. In addition, Bell (1972) found that the self-esteem of children placed in transition classes was lower than that of children who were not retained.

The use of standardized tests with young children for placement in pre–first grade or special education programs is a cause of major concern. One issue is the misuse of tests for placement purposes. The NAEYC position paper on the use of standardized tests urged test users to evaluate and carefully select tests only for the purposes for which they were intended (National Association for the Education of Young Children, 1988).

Meisels (1986) explained the differences between readiness tests and developmental screening tests. Readiness tests such as the *Metropolitan Readiness Test* (Nurss & McGauvran, 1976) and the *Gesell School Readiness Test* (Ilg & Ames, 1972) assess a child's current level of achievement and should not be used as a predictor of success in school. Shepard and Smith (1986) proposed that the *Gesell School Readiness Test* measures the same things as IQ tests, although the claim is made that it measures developmental age.

Meisels (1987) recommended the use of developmental screening tests to predict quickly whether a child could profit from a special education placement if such tests have predictive validity, developmental content, and normative standardization. Meisels considered the *Early Screening Inventory* (Meisels & Wiske, 1983), the *McCarthy Screening Test* (McCarthy, 1978), and the *Minneapolis Preschool Screening Test* (Lichtenstein, 1980) to have excellent reliability and predictive validity. Nevertheless, Meisels stated that developmental screening tests should be used to identify children who need further evaluation. The NAEYC position paper on the use of standardized tests (National Association for the Education of Young Children, 1988) further recommended that decisions on such issues as enrollment, retention, or placement in special classes should never be based on a single test score. Other sources of information, including systematic observation and samples of children's work, should be a part of the evaluation process.

Thurlow, O'Sullivan, and Ysseldyke (1986) also questioned the technical adequacy of tests being used to identify children for early education programs for handicapped children. They reported that a survey of model programs for such children found that only one-sixth of the tests used for screening purposes had appropriate validity, reliability, and norming samples.

The Need for Improvements in Standardized Tests

Not all writers would eliminate standardized tests. Cryan (1986) recommended the use of all types of informal and formal measurement strategies. When to use which type of measurement is the issue. Although he advocated teacher-designed evaluation strategies, Cryan also said that standardized tests are appropriate when there is a need to evaluate curriculum areas that are common to many groups of students.

Goodwin and Goodwin (1982) also indicated that there is a role for standardized tests in measuring young children. They believed that many early childhood educators are not opposed to the use of standardized tests per se, but rather to specific tests. According to these authors, teacher intuition for evaluation can be biased. Systematic measurement and evaluation can have advantages. Although they described the shortcomings of standardized tests used with young children, Goodwin and Goodwin asserted that more is needed than informal measures and teacher observations.

SUMMARY

Standardized tests, in spite of their shortcomings, are useful for test users. Because they have been carefully developed using a series of steps that ensure their dependability, educational institutions in particular use them to measure students' characteristics. Good standardized tests are normed using many individuals from various backgrounds who live in different parts of the United States. As a result, the tests also accurately measure the population to which they are given.

The normal curve is used as the standard reference for interpreting norm-referenced scores on the standardized test. The distribution of test scores can be compared to the normal curve and interpreted using percentiles, stanines, or standard scores. In this manner, individual performance on a test can be interpreted by comparison with the norms established by testing a sample group.

Although the process of developing a standardized test may seem to be unnecessarily tedious, good test design requires careful planning and attention to each step. The ultimate validity and reliability of the test result from attention to design details, beginning with the definition of the test's purpose and ending with the description of technical data about the test's construction in the users' manual.

Much is known about the development and use of standardized tests, particularly achievement tests; nevertheless, there is disagreement over whether and when they should be used as an educational tool. This is particularly true in formal testing of young children.

Standardized tests used with young children need continued improvement, but whether they are useful for developmentally appropriate educational programs for young children will not be easily determined. Test developers and early childhood specialists must continue to study the nature of assessment and evaluation and seek to improve strategies for effective measurement of young children.

Summary Statements

1. Standardized tests are characterized by consistency, validity, and uniformity in scoring and interpretation.
2. Standardized tests are designed to measure psychological characteristics.
3. Standardized tests may be administered either to individuals or to groups of children.
4. Test consistency, or reliability, may be calculated using test-retest, alternate-form, or split-half reliability estimates.
5. Test validity can be evaluated by an examination of criterion-related validity, content validity, and construct validity.
6. Standardized tests are constructed using a series of basic steps.
7. The norming of standardized tests provides test users with the means of comparing the performance of a student or groups of students with that of a reference group.
8. Scores on standardized tests are transformed using percentile rank norms, grade equivalent norms, and stanine norms.
9. Test performance is interpreted by transforming raw scores into standard scores, using the normal or bell-shaped curve as the measure of distribution.
10. The use of standardized tests in schools is controversial and subject to criticism.
11. Standardized tests have limitations that must be understood by test users.
12. Many early childhood educators believe that standardized tests should not be used with young children.
13. Limitations of standardized tests used with young children include poor validity and reliability, inappropriate use of test results, difficulties in test administration, and incomplete technical data in test manuals.

REVIEW QUESTIONS

1. What are the advantages of using tests that have been standardized?
2. What is meant by quantifiable scores?
3. Describe norm referencing.

4. Why does a test need to have validity? Reliability? Can you have one without the other?

5. Why is description of a test's purpose important? How does test purpose affect test design?

6. What are some factors test designers must consider before beginning to design a test?

7. What are the best formats to use with preschool children?

8. How are experimental test forms used?

9. What is meant by item tryout and analysis? What is accomplished during this procedure?

10. Discuss three types of item analysis.

11. What kinds of information are acquired when a test is standardized?

12. How is a norming population selected?

13. Explain content validity, criterion-related validity, and construct validity.

14. Explain alternate-form reliability, split-half reliability, and test-retest reliability.

15. Why does every test have a standard error of measurement?

16. Why is a normal curve used to chart the distribution of test scores?

17. What is the function of the mean on the normal curve?

18. How do standard deviations serve as reference points when interpreting test scores?

19. How are percentile ranks and stanines used with standardized test scores?

20. Why are Z scores and T scores useful?

21. What are some strengths of standardized tests?

22. How can standardized tests be criticized? Describe some weaknesses.

23. Why are standardized tests less effective for use with preschool children?

24. How do developmental problems affect test administration in early childhood classes?

25. Describe some ways that standardized tests designed for young children can be improved.

KEY TERMS

age norms	content validity
alternate-form reliability	criterion-related validity
concurrent validity	equivalent form
construct validity	grade equivalent

grade norms

group test

individual test

intelligence quotient

internal consistency

item analysis

mean

multiple-choice

normal distribution

norms

percentile

percentile rank

personality test

raw score

reliability

split-half reliability

standard deviation

standard error

standard score

stanine

T score

test-retest validity

true score

validity

Z score

REFERENCES

American Psychological Association. (1974). *Standards for educational and psychological tests and manuals.* Washington, D.C.: Author.

Bell, M. (1972). *A study of the readiness room program in a small school district in suburban Detroit, Michigan.* Unpublished dissertation, Wayne State University, Detroit.

Bracey, G. W. (1987). Measurement-driven instruction: Catchy phrase, dangerous practice. *Phi Delta Kappan, 68,* 683–686.

Brown, F. G. (1980). *Guidelines for test use: A commentary on the standards for educational and psychological tests.* Washington, D.C.: National Council on Measurement in Education.

Brown, F. G. (1983). *Principles of educational and psychological testing* (3rd ed.). New York: CBS College Publishing.

Buros, O. K. (1974). *Tests in print II.* Highland Park, NJ: Gryphon Press.

Buros, O. K. (Ed.). (1978). *The eighth mental measurements yearbook.* Highland Park, NJ: Gryphon Press.

Burrill, L. E. (1980). *How a standardized achievement test is built.* Test Service Notebook 125. New York: Psychological Corp.

Byrnes, D., & Yamamoto, K. (1984). *Grade retention: Views of parents, teachers and principals.* Logan: Utah State University Press.

Calfee, R. C. (1987). The school as a context for assessment of literacy. *The Reading Teacher, 40,* 738–743.

California Achievement Tests, Forms E and F Examination Materials. (1985). Monterey, CA: CTB/McGraw-Hill.

Cronbach, L. J. (1984). *Essentials of psychological testing.* New York: Harper & Row.

Cryan, J. R. (1986). Evaluation: Plague or promise? *Childhood Education, 62,* 344–350.

Dunn, L., & Dunn, L. (1981). *Manual forms L and M. Peabody Picture Vocabulary Test—Revised.* Circle Pines, MN: American Guidance Service.

Durkin, D. (1987). Testing in the kindergarten. *The Reading Teacher, 40,* 766–770.

Evans, E. D. (1974). Measurement practices in early childhood education. In R. W. Colvin & E. M. Zaffire (Eds.), *Preschool education: A handbook for the training of early childhood educators.* New York: Springer-Verlag.

Farr, R., & Carey, R. (1986). *Reading: What can be measured?* Newark, DE: International Reading Association.

Goodwin, W. L., & Goodwin, L. D. (1982). Measuring young children. In B. Spodek (Ed.), *Handbook of research in early childhood education.* (pp. 523–563). New York: Free Press.

Gredler, G. R. (1984). Transition classes: A viable alternative for the at-risk child? *Psychology in the Schools, 21,* 463–470.

Gronlund, N. E. (1985). *Measurement and evaluation in teaching.* New York: Macmillan.

Guilmet, G. M. (1983). The inappropriateness of standard testing in a culturally hetero-geneous milieu: A Navajo example. ERIC, ED 261830.

Holmes, C. T., & Matthews, K. M. (1984). The effects of nonpromotion on elementary and junior high school pupils: A meta-analysis. *Review of Educational Research, 54,* 225–236.

Ilg, F. L., & Ames, L. B. (1972). *School readiness.* New York: Harper & Row.

Ilg, F. L., Ames, L. B., & Gillespie, C. (1978). *Gesell School Readiness Test Kit.* Rosemont, NJ: Programs for Education Publishers.

Kamii, C. (1985a). Leading primary education toward excellence: Beyond worksheets and drill. *Young Children, 40,* 3–9.

Kamii, C. (1985b). *Young children reinvent arithmetic.* New York: Teachers College Press.

Kaplan, R. M., & Saccuzo, D. P. (1982). *Psychological testing principles, applications and issues.* Monterey, CA: Brooks/Cole.

Katz, L. (1985). Dispositions in early childhood education. *ERIC/EECE Bulletin, 18,* 1, 3.

Kaufman, A., & Kaufman, N. (1983). *K-ABC Kaufman Assessment Battery for Children Sampler manual.* Circle Pines, MN: American Guidance Service.

Keyser, D. J., & Sweetland, R. C. (1984–1987). *Test critiques* (Vols. I–VII). Kansas City, MO: Test Corporation of America.

Lichtenstein, R. (1980). *The Minneapolis Preschool Screening Inventory.* Minneapolis: Minne-apolis Public Schools.

Madden, R., & Gardner, E. F. (1969 and 1971). *Stanford Early Achievement Test: Directions for administering. Levels I and II.* New York: Harcourt Brace Jovanovich.

McCarthy, D. (1978). *The McCarthy Screening Test.* New York: New York Psychological Corp.

Mehrens, W. A., & Lehmann, I. J. (1984). *Measurement and evaluation in education and psychology.* New York: Holt, Rinehart & Winston.

Meisels, S. J. (1986). Testing four- and five-year olds: Response to Salzer and to Shepard and Smith. *Educational Leadership, 44,* 90–92.

Meisels, S. J. (1987). Uses and abuses of developmental screening and school readiness testing. *Young Children, 42,* 4–6, 68–73.

Meisels, S. J., & Wiske, M. S. (1983). *The Early Screening Inventory.* New York: Teachers College Press.

National Association for the Education of Young Children. (1986). Position statement on developmentally appropriate practice in early childhood programs serving children from birth through age 8. *Young Children, 41,* 3–19.

National Association for the Education of Young Children. (1988). Position statement on standardized testing of young children 3 through 8 years of age. *Young Children, 43,* 42–47.

National Education Association. (1972). Moratorium on standard testing. *Today's Education, 61,* 41.

National Education Association. (1977). *Standardized testing issues: Teachers' perspectives.* Washington, D.C.: Author.

National School Boards Association. (1977). *Standardized achievement testing.* Washington, D.C.: Author.

Nurss, J. R., & McGauvran, M. E. (1976). *Metropolitan Readiness Tests.* New York: Harcourt Brace Jovanovich.

Oakland, T., & Laosa, L. M. (1977). Professional, legislative, and judicial influences on psychoeducational assessment practices in schools. In T. Oakland (Ed.), *Psychological and educational assessment of minority children.* New York: Bruner/Mazel.

Perrone, V. (1976–1978). *On standardized testing and evaluation.* Association for Childhood Education International. Reprint CE-9/1976–78. Wheaton, MD: Association for Childhood Education International.

Perrone, V. (1981). Testing, testing and more testing. *Childhood Education, 58,* 76–80.

Popham, W. J. (1987). The merits of measurement-driven instruction. *Phi Delta Kappan, 68,* 679–682.

Salmon-Cox, L. (1981). Teachers and standardized achievement tests: What's really happening? *Phi Delta Kappan, 62,* 631–633.

Seashore, H. G. (1980). *Methods of expressing test scores.* Test Service Notebook 148. New York: Psychological Corp.

Shepard, L. A., & Smith, M. L. (1986). Synthesis of research on school readiness and kindergarten retention. *Education Leadership, 44,* 78–86.

Teale, W. (1988). Developmentally appropriate assessment of reading and writing in the early childhood classroom. *Elementary School Journal, 89,* 173–183.

Teale, W., Hiebert, E., & Chittenden, E. (1987). Assessing young children's literacy development. *The Reading Teacher, 40,* 772–776.

Thurlow, M. L., O'Sullivan, P. J., & Ysseldyke, J. E. (1986). Early screening for special education: How accurate? *Educational Leadership, 44,* 93–95.

Valencia, S., & Pearson, P. (1987). Reading assessment: Time for a change. *The Reading Teacher, 40,* 726–732.

Weber, G. (1977). *Uses and abuses of standardized testing in the schools.* Washington, D.C.: Council for Basic Education.

4
Using and Reporting
Standardized Test Results

Tests are administered to young children to acquire beneficial information about them. In Chapter 3, we learned how standardized tests are planned, designed, and standardized. We also considered how the normal curve is used as a reference for translating test scores and comparing individual scores with a norm.

In this chapter, we learn more about using information from children's test scores. In the process of standardizing a test, developers establish the norms that make test score interpretation useful. We not only take a more detailed look at norm-referenced tests, we also study how another type of standardized test—the criterion-referenced test—is used to meet the learning needs of young children. Group test scores can be used to analyze and improve curriculum and instruction at various levels within a school district; individual test scores can be used by the classroom teacher to organize appropriate learning experiences for individual students or the class as a whole.

We will also discuss now how individual and group test results are used to report student progress and program effectiveness. Test results are important to teachers, school district administrators, parents, and school boards. They are reported to each in a context that provides meaningful interpretation of the test. Finally, we will consider the disadvantages as well as the advantages of using norm- and criterion-referenced tests with young children.

USES OF NORM-REFERENCED AND CRITERION-REFERENCED TESTS

Distinctions Between Norm-Referenced and Criterion-Referenced Tests

Norm-referenced and criterion-referenced tests are both standardized instruments. Some standardized tests are designed for norm-referenced results and others for criterion-referenced reporting. The current trend is to design tests that are both norm and criterion referenced. The two types of tests have different purposes, and test items are used differently when measuring student learning or achievement. **Norm-referenced tests** provide information on how the performance of the individual compares with that of others. The individual's standing is compared with that of a known group. The student's percentile rank is obtained to determine the relative standing in a norm group by recording what percentage of the group obtained the same score or a lower score.

In contrast, **criterion-referenced tests** provide information on how the individual performed on some standard or objective. These test results allow users to interpret what an individual can do without considering the performance of others. Criterion-referenced tests are designed to measure the results of instruction; they determine the student's performance on specific behavioral or instructional objectives (Wilson, 1980). Gronlund (1981) described the difference between the two types of tests as the ends of a continuum: "The norm-referenced test, at one end, emphasizes *discrimination* among pupils, and criterion-referenced test, at the other end, emphasizes *description* of performance" (p. 15).

Norm-referenced and criterion-referenced tests have certain characteristics in common. Gronlund (1981) described those common characteristics as follows:

1. Both require a relevant and representative sample of test items.
2. Both require specification of the achievement domain to be measured.
3. Both use the same type of test items.
4. Both use the same rules for item writing (except for item difficulty).
5. Both are judged by the same qualities of goodness (validity and reliability).
6. Both are useful in educational measurement. (p. 14)

Both tests measure what students have learned; nevertheless, the objectives for measurement are different. The norm-referenced test is broad in content. There are many aspects of the content to be measured. Because the test is concerned with overall achievement, only a small sample of behaviors for each objective can be assessed. On the criterion-referenced test, the focus is on mastery of objectives. There are many test questions for each objective to determine whether the objective has been mastered.

An achievement test in mathematics provides a good example. The norm-referenced test for the first grade may have items on addition, subtraction, sets, and all other areas that are included in the mathematics curriculum. Test items are written to sample the student's overall performance in first-grade mathematics. On the criterion-referenced test, student performance on individual curriculum objectives is important. Test items are written to measure whether the child has mastered a particular learning objective in subtraction, addition, or other components of the mathematics curriculum (Goodwin & Goodwin, 1982).

Another difference between norm-referenced and criterion-referenced tests also relates to differences in test items. In a norm-referenced instrument, test items must cover a wide range of difficulty. Because the test is intended to discriminate between the performance of students and groups of students, the difficulty of test items will range above the grade level for which the test is intended. Test items designed primarily for criterion-referenced purposes are written specifically for learning tasks. Easy items are not omitted, and the intent is to evaluate how well the student has learned the objectives for one grade level (Wilson, 1980).

New standardized tests have been developed with dual referencing; that is, they are designed for both norm-referenced and criterion-referenced assessment. Although it is difficult to have a single test that is equally well designed for both types of measurement, obtaining both kinds of performance results is helpful to educators. Compromises in test construction are offset by more effective use of the test (Gronlund, 1981). It should also be noted that some criterion-referenced tests have not been standardized. This does not imply that they are not well designed and useful, but readers should be aware of this condition.

Uses of Norm-Referenced Measurement with Preschool Children

Norm-referenced test scores are used to measure individual achievement within a designated group. Norms are not standards to be reached; they are numerical descriptions of the test performance of a group of students. Norms can be established at a national level or at a local level. Norm-referenced tests are commonly used to measure school achievement, intelligence, aptitude, and personality traits.

Formal tests are administered at the preschool level to identify children who need or can benefit from special instruction, as well as to determine the success of an early childhood program.

Measures of intelligence such as the *Wechsler Preschool and Primary Scale of Intelligence* (Wechsler, 1967) and the *Wechsler Intelligence Scale for Children-Revised* (Wechsler, 1974) are norm-referenced instruments that allow test examiners to differentiate the skills or knowledge of the students who are tested. Preschool intelligence tests may be used to identify students for a class for learning-disabled children, as well as to qualify children for a preschool gifted program. They may also be used with any children for whom an intelligence measure is deemed necessary.

Norm-referenced tests are used with preschool children to measure their present level of knowledge, skills, or performance. In federally funded programs such as Head Start, a norm-referenced measure may be used to evaluate the learning acquired by the children as a result of the program. The *Peabody Picture Vocabulary Test-Revised* (Dunn & Dunn, 1981) provides a measure for language development. The *Boehm Test of Basic Concepts* (Boehm, 1971) and the *Learning Accomplishment Profile* (Sanford, 1974) assess the child's abilities and skills, including the acquisition of concepts.

Uses of Norm-Referenced Measurement with School-Age Children

When children enter primary school, achievement tests are the most frequently administered norm-referenced test. Locally developed achievement tests, as well as state and national tests, can be given to measure and analyze individual and group performance resulting from the educational program. Children who are experiencing difficulties in school are evaluated with screening and diagnostic tests, but all students take achievement tests as early as kindergarten, more frequently beginning in first grade.

Norm-referenced test results are used for more general comparisons of group test results. One such use is to assess achievement level in subject areas. The achievement of a single class in a school, all classes of a certain grade level in the school, all schools with the grade level in a school district, and all schools within a state with that grade level can be studied to determine general progress in one or more subject areas. The results of batteries of tests can be analyzed for trends in achievement.

In a similar type of analysis, components of an instructional program can be studied using group test scores. If a new instructional program is to be tried, or if an existing method is to be evaluated to decide whether changes are needed, an achievement test can be used to investigate the effectiveness of the program. Particular areas of weakness and strength can be pinpointed, and decisions and plans can be made to improve weak components in the curriculum.

Uses of Criterion-Referenced Measurement with Preschool Children

Criterion-referenced test scores are used to describe individual performance on specific objectives. Criterion-referenced measures deemphasize distinctions between individual performances; rather, they indicate whether the individual has mastered the objectives that were tested. Criterion-referenced tests are used for developmental screening, diagnostic evaluation, and instructional planning.

In the preschool years, developmental and diagnostic assessment are the criterion-referenced tests used most frequently. Although **developmental screening** is primarily used to identify children who might profit from early education intervention or from special services before kindergarten or first grade, it is also used as a checkpoint for children who are developing normally. Figure 4.1 is an example of a developmental scale to measure social development (Alpern, Boll, & Shearer, 1984).

Many screening tests have been developed as a result of the Education for All Handicapped Children Act (Public Law 94-142), which required handicapped

TODDLER II: 2–1 to 2–6 years
(25–30 months)
Basal Credit 30 months

Does the child name his/her own sex or tell the sex of others? Child may pass by showing he/she knows that certain clothes, activities, or toys usually go with one sex or another.

Does the child like to help the parents around the house? Does the child enjoy such activities as picking things up from the floor, putting raked leaves in a basket, dusting, setting or clearing the table?

TODDLER III: 2–7 to 3–0 years
(31–36 months)
Basal Credit 36 months

Does the child follow the rules in group games run by an adult? Such rules might mean being able to sit in a circle, follow directions, imitate a leader, or do the same things as the rest of the group.

Is the child able to take turns? Although some help may be needed, the child understands the idea of waiting for someone else to go first *and* allows others to go first 75% of the time

PRESCHOOLER I: 3–1 to 3–6 years
(37–42 months)
Basal Credit 42 months

Does the child play group games with other children such as tag, hide-and-seek, hopscotch, jump rope, or marbles without needing constant supervision by an adult?

Is the child able to keep "working" for at least *30 minutes* with a similar-aged child on a *single task* such as block building, sand or mud play, or playing store, school, or house?

PRESCHOOLER II: 3–7 to 4–6 years
(43–54 months)
Basal Credit 54 months

Does the child draw a person so that an adult could tell what was drawn? It need not be a whole person, but there should be a head *and* body, *or* a head *and* eyes, nose, or mouth which any adult could recognize.

Is the child allowed to play in his/her own neighborhood without being watched by an adult? This does not mean the child is allowed to cross the street alone.

FIGURE 4.1
Developmental Profile II (DPII)
Social Developmental Age Scale

Copyright © 1984 by Western Psychological Services. Excerpted from the *Developmental Profile II* and reprinted by permission of the publisher, Western Psychological Services, 12031 Wilshire Boulevard, Los Angeles, California 90025.

children to be placed in the "least restrictive environment" possible. As described by Meisels, "Early childhood developmental screening is a brief assessment procedure designed to identify children who, because of the risk of a possible learning problem or handicapping condition, should proceed to a more intensive level of diagnostic assessment" (1985, 1). Thus developmental surveys assess affective, cognitive, and psychomotor characteristics to determine whether further testing and evaluation are needed to identify disabilities and strategies for remediation.

Many screening tests have been developed for the preschool child. The *Denver Developmental Screening Test* (Frankenburg, Dodds, Fandal, Kajuk, and Cohr, 1975) is commonly used by pediatricians and other medical professionals. The *Early Screening Inventory* (Meisels & Wiske, 1983) and the *McCarthy Screening Test* (McCarthy, 1972) are also used for screening purposes. Figure 4.2 shows some of the criterion-referenced screening items on the *Early Screening Inventory* (Meisels & Wiske, 1983).

When children have a developmental problem that should be investigated beyond screening procedures, **diagnostic evaluation** may be needed. The purposes of this assessment are to identify a child's strengths and weaknesses and, ultimately, to suggest strategies for remediation. An example of a diagnostic evaluation instrument that can be used with preschool children is the *Kaufman Assessment Battery for Children* (Kaufman & Kaufman, 1983).

Uses of Criterion-Referenced Measurement with School-Age Children

Diagnostic evaluation measures are also used with school-age children. Intelligence batteries and diagnostic tests in academic content areas are used with students who demonstrate learning difficulties. In addition, criterion-referenced results are used for instructional planning with children at all levels of learning needs and achievement.

Criterion-referenced scores on achievement tests are used to describe individual performance. Reports of individual performance are then used for instructional planning. Individual performance can also be used in teaching groups of children with the same instructional needs.

Mastery testing is a common criterion-referenced measure. Instructional objectives are assessed. When mastery on a test objective has been achieved, instruction proceeds with a new objective. In the case of an achievement test, performance results may be charted to show which objectives have been mastered by the test taker and which ones need further attention. This result can be used in planning instruction for a group of students. In a similar manner, individualized instruction can be initiated as a result of criterion-referenced test results. Figure 4.3 gives the prereading behavioral objectives that are assessed on the *California-Achievement Test (CAT) (1977)*.

In **individualized instruction,** students are taught singly based on personal needs, rather than in large groups. Instead of planning learning activities for the

Appendix A

ESI

Early Screening Inventory

S. J. Meisels and M. S. Wiske

SCORE SHEET

Child's name _____   School _____

Date of screening _____ / _____ / _____   Teacher _____
                   year   month   day

Date of birth _____ / _____ / _____   Screener _____
              year   month   day

Current age _____ / _____   Sex: male ____ female ____   Parent questionnaire completed? yes ____ no ____
             years   months

I. INITIAL SCREENING ITEMS	Pass	Fail	Refuse	Total Points Possible	Total Points Received	Comments
A. Draw a Person (5 parts)				1		
B. Name or Other Letters						
II. VISUAL-MOTOR/ADAPTIVE						
A. Copy Forms						
1. Copy ○				1		
2. Copy +				1		
3. Copy □				1		
4. Copy △				1		

ISBN 0-8077-6080-3 (kit)
ISBN 0-8077-6083-8 (refill)

II. VISUAL-MOTOR/ADAPTIVE (continued) B. Visual Sequential Memory	Pass	Fail	Refuse	Total Points Possible	Total Points Received	Comments
1. + ○				0		
2. ○ + □				1		
or + □ ○ (if fail)				1		
C. Block Building						
Gate (screen)				3		
or Gate (imitate) (if fail)				2		
or Bridge (screen) (if fail)				1		
III. LANGUAGE AND COGNITION						
A. Number Concept						
1. Count 10 blocks				2		
or Count 5 blocks (if fail)				1		
2. How many altogether?				1		

B. Verbal Expression	Name	Color	Shape	Use	Other	Comments
Ball						
Button						
Block						
Car						

Total Score for Verbal Expression _____   Points Received (0-3)

0-5 = 0 pts.;
6-20 = 1 pt;
21-35 = 2 pts.;
36+ = 3 pts.

FIGURE 4.2

Early Screening Inventory: example of a developmental screening instrument

Source: Meisels and Wiske, 1983.

Test	Category Objective
Listening for information	1. School vocabulary 2. Space/direction/location 3. Relationships—facts/concepts
Letter forms	4. Match uppercase/lowercase
Letter names	5. Recognize uppercase/lowercase
Letter sounds	6. Long vowels (picture/letter) 7. Short vowels (picture/letter) 8. Single consonants (picture/letter)
Visual discrimination	9. Match shapes 10. Match three-letter words 11. Match five- and six-letter words
Sound matching	12. Identical words (oral) 13. Medial short vowels (oral words) 14. Initial consonants (oral words) 15. Final consonants (oral words) 16. Consonant clusters/digraphs (oral words)

FIGURE 4.3
California Achievement Test: examples of objectives used in a criterion-referenced test
Source: California *Achievement Tests: Tests Coordinator's Handbook, Forms C and D,* 1977.

class as a whole, the teacher diversifies instruction based on the progress of each student. Instructional groups of different sizes are formed, and the pace of instruction is differentiated based on individual progress. Criterion-referenced tests are one source of information for individualized instruction.

Minimum-competency testing also utilizes criterion-referenced test results. In **minimum-competency testing** a minimum standard is set regarding competence in achieving test objectives. Individual test scores are interpreted to screen for test takers who have reached or exceeded the established level of competency. Many states are instituting minimum-competency tests for students at the elementary school level that determine promotion or retention.

On a larger scale, criterion-referenced test scores are used for broad surveys of educational accomplishment. Group achievement on a local, state, or national level is assessed to better understand educational progress. Achievement of very large groups of children is analyzed to assess strengths and weaknesses in instruction beyond the level of an individual school district. For example, students tested on a national achievement test in reading were found to be stronger in word identification skills than in comprehension skills. When such information is acquired at a state or national level, curriculum resources and teaching practices can be investigated to correct the problem. In addition to the *California Achievement Test,* other achievement tests that include criterion-referenced information are the

Comprehensive Test of Basic Skills (1974) and the *Stanford Early Achievement Test* (Madden & Gardner, 1969, 1971).

ADVANTAGES AND DISADVANTAGES OF USING NORM-REFERENCED AND CRITERION-REFERENCED TESTS WITH YOUNG CHILDREN

In Chapter 3, some of the concerns about using standardized tests with young children were discussed. Particularly controversial is the practice of using developmental tests to postpone kindergarten attendance or to require a child to spend 2 years in school before entering first grade (Durkin, 1987). When considering norm-referenced and criterion-referenced tests specifically, there are advantages when the correct kind of test is administered for an appropriate purpose.

Developmental tests are beneficial when they are used to screen preschool children who are at risk for academic failure in elementary school. Screening tests can quickly identify such children and can indicate whether a child should undergo more intensive evaluation to identify and remediate a learning handicap (Meisels, 1985). The earlier such handicaps are identified and intervention is begun, the more likely it is that the child will be able to overcome the handicap before entering elementary school.

Norm-referenced and criterion-referenced achievement tests can provide valuable information regarding the effectiveness of curriculum and instruction. At the beginning of the school year, such tests can show what children know in relation to an instructional program (Durkin, 1987). Likewise, achievement tests administered at the end of the school year can demonstrate how well children learned the content of the program. Teachers can use the test results to determine how to reteach or change program content and/or instructional methods. In other words, teachers can use test results to evaluate their program and make changes to meet the instructional needs of their students more effectively. Goodwin and Goodwin (1982) stated that for many early childhood educators, instructional planning was the only justification for testing young children.

Unfortunately, when Durkin (1987) studied the testing practices of 15 school districts, she did not find that test results were used to determine the appropriateness of the instructional program. To the contrary, programs were "cast in stone" (p. 769), and children had to adapt to the programs. La Crosse (1970) reported that teachers relied more on their intuition than on measurement data.

As discussed in Chapter 3, Meisels (1987) was particularly concerned about the misuse of screening and readiness tests with young children. He stated that readiness tests should be used for curriculum planning, but that they are frequently used as developmental screening tests to identify children in need of intervention or special services. Meisels pointed out that individual readiness tests do not have a strong predictive relationship to outcome measures.

There are other disadvantages or difficulties in using norm-referenced and criterion-referenced tests. Screening tests for early identification and possible

USING ACHIEVEMENT TEST RESULTS TO IMPROVE TEACHING AND LEARNING

The school board in Lucky analyzed the yearly report on school achievement in their community. Results indicated that students achieved at the national norm through the third grade, but thereafter scores tended to drop off steadily among some groups of students. Minority student scores dropped more significantly than the scores of Anglo students. Students from lower-income homes did less well than middle-class students.

The teachers in the elementary schools studied the criterion-referenced test results to discover whether there were certain objectives on which the results were weak. It was determined that there were consistent indicators of weakness in reading comprehension and problem solving in mathematics. As a group, students in the school district were stronger in word attack skills in reading and computation in mathematics than they were in higher-order skills that involved analysis and synthesis.

A committee of teachers at each grade level was assigned to search instructional resources to find supplementary materials that would strengthen teaching in those areas. The committees were particularly interested in finding materials that would involve the students in applying what they were learning in mathemat-ics and allow students to engage in meaningful reading experiences.

The grade-level committees first searched through reading and math materials that were available in their own classrooms. They then surveyed materials that were available through the school district's central resource center. Finally, they traveled to a regional educational service center. There they were assisted by an educational consultant in locating additional resources that addressed their students' needs in mathematics and reading. The consultant also worked with the committees in designing workshops to share materials and teaching strategies with the other teachers at each grade level.

The second year after the supplementary materials were included, a small improvement was noted in the test scores. There was another gain in the third year.

Now, each year, a committee of teachers studies test results to see where the students are encountering difficulty in order to determine whether the instructional program should be modified. They are especially attentive to those students who are likely to have lower scores. The school board is pleased with the steady improvement in elementary achievement scores.

reversal of developmental disabilities have been used in compliance with the mandates of PL 94-142. Nevertheless, Goodwin and Driscoll (1980) felt that implementation of the law has been difficult.

Some of the problems occurred because the law failed to specify how the screening was to be conducted. As a result, procedures vary and screening and diagnosis are often combined into one process which can cause ambiguity and confusion.

Other disadvantages are that well-trained personnel are not always available for screening and diagnosis. In addition, there is no consistency in classification and remediation of disabled children who move from state to state. Finally, although many tests have been developed for screening and diagnosis, their quality varies.

MISUSE OF ACHIEVEMENT TEST RESULTS

Livingston School District, a large urban district, implemented a program for gifted and talented students in response to a mandate by the state education agency. Because funds were very limited, only a small number of the students who were eligible could be served at each grade level. To be fair to the students and avoid complaints from parents, it was decided to use achievement test results as the main criterion for selection. Students' names were ranked in alphabetical order according to their percentile rank on the test.

In the second grade, 15 students were selected. Freddie Marcus was 16th on the list. Although he had the same percentile rank as both students above him on the list, he was not included in the program because his last name fell later in the alphabet than theirs.

When the second-grade teachers received the results of the test and the subsequent list of students selected for the program, Freddie's teacher questioned why he was not included. The building principal did not feel that she could be flexible in determining the number of stu-

dents who would be served and decided against including Freddie.

At the next monthly meeting of building teachers, Freddie's teacher asked to discuss the selection process for the gifted and talented program. She questioned the use of a single standardized test to select students, particularly because characteristics of giftedness and different kinds of talent were to be considered. She also asked that flexibility be built into the selection process to include students like Freddie.

The building principal formed a committee of teachers to study the problem and to suggest methods for improving the program and the selection process within the budget limitations. The committee offered a process of teacher observation and questionnaires to be filled in by parents to be added to the standardized test in selecting children for the program. The committee also suggested that the teacher trained for the gifted and talented program provide classroom teachers with suggestions about providing experiences for a broader group of students within their own classrooms.

When and how norm- and criterion-referenced tests should be used with young children is a current issue facing educators who are associated with early childhood programs. Goodlad, Klein, and Novotney (1973) determined that most early childhood education programs do not use a systematic program for evaluation. In the Position Statement on Developmentally Appropriate Practice in Early Childhood Programs Serving Children from Birth Through Age 8 (National Association for the Education of Young Children, 1986), the following statement was made regarding evaluation or assessment of young children:

A. Decisions that have a major impact on children such as enrollment, retention, or placement are made on the basis of a single developmental screening device, but consider other relevant information, particularly observation by teachers and parents. . . . (p. 16)

Obviously, educators in early childhood education need to be more informed about the use of standardized tests and informal measures for the evaluation of young children. Informal methods, including observation, will be addressed in Chapter 5.

REPORTING STANDARDIZED TEST RESULTS

When a standardized test has been administered and scored, and individual and group scores have been interpreted, test users can use the information to report not only to professionals within the school district but also to the parents of the students. Reporting originates with individual test results, which are then combined and recombined with the scores of other individuals to form class, school, and district reports.

Individual Test Record

The individual test record (Figure 4.4) is from the *Stanford Diagnostic Reading Test* (Karlsen & Gardner, 1984). The hypothetical student is Robin J. Phillips, who is in the third grade. The test was administered in October, the second month of the school year. Because the SDRT is both a norm-referenced and a criterion-referenced test, both kinds of scores are reported. In Figure 4.4, norm-referenced scores are located under the heading "Subtests and Totals"; the criterion-referenced or content-referenced information is presented under the heading "Skills Analysis."

Norm-Referenced and Criterion-Referenced Scores

The Instructional Placement Report includes the subtests or content areas of the test battery. The subtests are Auditory Vocabulary, Auditory Discrimination, Phonetic Analysis, Structural Analysis, and Reading Comprehension. Within each subtest the raw score, scaled score, and grade equivalent are reported. The **scaled score** is a continuous score over all grade levels. It indicates the student's progress on the continuum for each category. In addition the stanine(s), percentile rank (PR), and percentile bands are included for each subtest.

The "Skills Analysis" section of the test record shows Robin's achievement in individual skills categories within the subtests. The skills measured on the SDRT are Vocabulary, Auditory Discrimination, Phonetic Analysis, Structural Analysis, and Reading Comprehension. Robin's teacher, Adrienne Kirby, can study Robin's progress in the skill categories by comparing his raw scores with the number of correct responses possible for each skill. Further, information is provided in the Progress Indicator (PI) columns. If the score is under the plus (+) side of the column, it indicates that the raw score is at or above the PI cutoff. If the score is under the minus (−) side of the column, it means that Robin scored below the PI cutoff. The PI cutoff score provides additional data on how the PI decision is determined.

Class Reports

Individual Class Records for students in a classroom can be analyzed for a report on the achievement of the class as a whole (Figure 4.5). The class record sheet of the Stanford Diagnostic Reading Test (SDRT) (Karlsen, Madden, & Gardner, 1976)

SDRT
STANFORD DIAGNOSTIC READING TEST
3rd EDITION © Copyright © 1984 by Harcourt Brace Jovanovich, Inc.

THE PSYCHOLOGICAL CORPORATION

COPY 1

INDIVIDUAL DIAGNOSTIC REPORT

FOR

ROBIN J PHILLIPS

TEACHER	ADRIENNE KIRBY	GRADE 3
SCHOOL	LAKESIDE ELEM	LEVEL GREEN FORM G
SYSTEM	NEWTOWN	NORMS GRADE 3 FALL
TEST DATE	10/84	

© HARCOURT BRACE JOVANOVICH, INC.

LEGEND
PR = PERCENTILE RANK
S = STANINE
RS = RAW SCORE
NP = NUMBER POSSIBLE
NCE = NORMAL CURVE EQUIVALENT

SUBTESTS AND TOTALS

	RAW SCORE	SCALED SCORE	GRADE EQUIV	NATIONAL S	PR
AUDITORY VOCABULARY	29	560	2.9	5	45
AUDITORY DISCRIMINATION	19	537	1.9	4	25
PHONETIC ANALYSIS	16	513	1.2	3	12
STRUCTURAL ANALYSIS	31	514	2.0	4	23
READING COMPREHENSION	26	523	2.0	3	19
SDRT TOTAL	121	529	2.0	3	20

NATIONAL PERCENTILE BANDS
1   5   10   20   30   40   50   60   70   80   90   95   99

SKILLS ANALYSIS

	ITEMS NP	RS	PI	PI +/-
VOCABULARY	40	29		
READING & LITERATURE	18	13	11	>>>
MATH & SCIENCE	12	8	7	>>
SOCIAL STUDIES & THE ARTS	10	8	5	
AUDITORY DISCRIMINATION	30	19		
CONSONANTS	15	8	9	
SINGLE CONSONANTS	5	3	3	>
CONSONANT CLUSTERS	5	3	3	>
CONSONANT DIGRAPHS	5	3	3	>
VOWELS	15	11	9	
SHORT VOWELS	5	4	3	>
LONG VOWELS	5	4	3	>
OTHER VOWELS	5	3	3	>
PHONETIC ANALYSIS	30	16		
CONSONANTS	15	10	9	
SINGLE CONSONANTS	5	4	3	>
CONSONANT CLUSTERS	5	4	3	>
CONSONANT DIGRAPHS	5	2	3	>
VOWELS	15	6	7	
SHORT VOWELS	5	3	3	>
LONG VOWELS	5	2	2	>
OTHER VOWELS	5	1	2	>

PI = PROGRESS INDICATOR CUTOFF SCORE; + = AT OR ABOVE; - = BELOW

SKILLS ANALYSIS

	ITEMS NP	RS	PI	PI +/-
STRUCTURAL ANALYSIS	48	31		
WORD DIVISION				
COMPOUND WORDS	24	13	15	>
AFFIXES	6	5	6	>
SYLLABLES	9	4	6	>
BLENDING	24	18	15	
COMPOUND WORDS	6	6	5	>
AFFIXES	9	7	6	>
SYLLABLES	9	5	4	>
READING COMPREHENSION	48	26		
LITERAL	24	15	14	>
INFERENTIAL	24	11	11	>

INSTRUCTIONAL GROUP 2: DECODING

This pupil earned comparatively low scores on one or more of the decoding subtests (Auditory Discrimination, Phonetic Analysis, and Structural Analysis). Decoding has to do with the ability to translate letters and patterns of letters into the sounds they represent and with the ability to analyze word parts. Since pupils in Group 2 are probably having difficulty with the decoding skills, progress in reading is likely to improve once attention is given to these skills. Suggestions for developing the decoding skills of pupils in Group 2 are given in the SDRT Manual for Interpreting and Handbook of Instructional Techniques and Materials.

PROCESS NO 02-000064-001

FIGURE 4.4
Examples of individual test records: norm-referenced scores and criterion-referenced scores   *Source:* Stanford Diagnostic Reading Test: Third Edition.
Copyright © 1984 by Harcourt Brace Jovanovich, Inc.   Reprinted by permission. All rights reserved.

lists the norm-referenced and criterion-referenced scores for each student. In the class report, the teacher can study the norm-referenced achievement scores for each student. In addition, the criterion-referenced information shows the number of students who scored above or below the PI cutoff in each skill category. The teacher can study the Progress Indicators in each Skill Domain category to determine which students need additional instruction in that category. If large numbers of students show nonmastery of certain skills, the curriculum can be studied to make appropriate changes in instruction.

School and District Reports

Summaries of class reports can be grouped to form school and district reports. Both norm-referenced and criterion-referenced information can be organized in a useful form for building principals, school district evaluators, superintendents, and governing boards. Achievement reports can be studied by grade level across a school or among all the schools in the district serving a grade level. Instructional strengths and weaknesses can be analyzed by content areas, as well as by school or by grade level. Over several years, achievement can be compared to determine long-term improvement or decline in achievement. Each type of analysis must take into account the error of measurement on the test so that realistic conclusions are drawn from the study of test results.

REPORTING TEST RESULTS TO PARENTS

Parents have the right to know about their child's performance in school, and schools have the responsibility to keep parents informed. One method used to report student learning is the standardized achievement tests. The school should report the test results in a manner that is helpful to the parents.

Statistical data that are part of standardized test reports can be confusing to parents. Because of the seeming complexity of test reports, it is important to give parents an opportunity to meet with the teacher for an explanation of their child's test results. In a parent–teacher conference, test results can be discussed.

The classroom teacher has the major responsibility for explaining standardized test results to parents. The teacher not only knows the child from working with her each day, but is also aware of the kinds of information individual parents will understand and want to acquire. Because parents differ in their educational background and experience with standardized tests, teachers often find it helpful to explain the value, as well as the limitations of the test scores. For some parents, the teacher will describe the test results in terms of what the child can and cannot do, rather than in terms of numerical scores. Parents may also benefit from knowing why the test was chosen and how the results will be used.

It may be helpful for parents to understand how the criterion-referenced test results may be used to plan appropriate learning experiences for their child. For

Stanford Diagnostic Reading Test

Teacher MARY GERARD
School UPPER CITY ELEM
System SMALLTOWN INDEPENDENT

Grade 2
Date of Testing 10/06/76
Level RED   **Form** A   **Norms Used** GRADE 2.0-2.5

Page 02 of 11   **for this CLASS**
Process No. 000-0000-000

THE PSYCHOLOGICAL CORPORATION   Ψ Data Services

SDRT INSTRUCTIONAL PLACEMENT REPORT

GROUP 2

SUBTEST AND TOTAL SCORES

LIST SEQUENCE — ALPHABETIC WITHIN GROUP

NAME: AGE (YRS/MOS) / OTHER INFORMATION

Subtests: AUDITORY DISCRIMINATION · PHONETIC ANALYSIS · AUDITORY VOCABULARY · WORD READING · READING COMPREHENSION · COMPREHEN TOTAL

Students listed:
DANVERS JOHN M 7-04N;
ELLIS LINDA 7-06N;
FARGO WARREN Z 7-10N;
MAYO HELMUT R 7-11N;
OLSEN DICK P 8-00N;
PETERS MARY 6-02N;
AHAB MARK C 7-07N;
BOWERS JIM C 7-05N;
CICERO ANNA M 7-00N

LEGEND: RS = Raw Score (Number Right) · PR = Percentile Rank · S = Stanine · SS = Scaled Score · GE = Grade Equivalent

N = National Norms   L = Local Norms

SKILL DOMAIN ANALYSIS

AUDITORY DISCRIMINATION · PHONETIC ANALYSIS · STRUCTURAL ANALYSIS · READING COMPREHENSION

PI = Progress Indicator
+ means Raw Score at or above PI Cutoff
– means Raw Score below PI Cutoff

See back for aids for interpretation.

FIGURE 4.5
Example of a class report

Source: Stanford Diagnostic Reading Test: Third Edition. Copyright © 1984 by Harcourt Brace Jovanovich, Inc. Reprinted by permission. All rights reserved.

73

example, the teacher may use test results to suggest activities that the parent can use to help the child.

The teacher may also wish to discuss the comparison of test scores of various children, particularly siblings. Parents will be reassured to know that individual differences in test scores result from many variables. Comparing test scores made by different children is neither accurate nor useful.

Once children enter the primary grades, parents are eager to know how well their child is progressing and whether the child is achieving as well as he should be at that grade level. Analysis of the results of a standardized achievement test can provide the information parents need; however, care should be used in interpreting standard scores and other norms used to report the test results. Grade equivalents, percentile ranks, and stanines are the norms most commonly reported to parents from standardized achievement tests. Each can be confusing and must be interpreted carefully so that parents will not misunderstand the implications of the information.

Grade Equivalents

Some test publishers recommend that grade equivalents not be used to report to parents because they are the most easily misunderstood norm. If they are reported, parents should be given a complete explanation of their meaning.

Parents can understand that a grade equivalent is the grade level reported, in years and months, of the average or mean score of the norming group. Comparing individual test scores to the grade equivalent scores is one way to determine whether a student scored above or below the mean. Parents can misunderstand that grade equivalent scores are not an indicator of the grade-level work that the child is capable of doing. Rather, these scores indicate that the child made the same number of correct responses as the children in the norming group at the grade level in the grade equivalent score. The test score indicates whether the child performed above or below average, but it does not show grade placement in school. Because parents find it difficult to understand the norm comparison made with grade equivalents, percentile ranks and stanines are more effectively used in reporting student performance.

Percentile Ranks

To understand percentile rank, the parent must first learn about the norming sample used to standardize the test. Then they can understand that their child's percentile score indicates the percentage of students in the norm group who got the same or a lower score on the test. Parents also need to recognize that the percentile rank has nothing to do with the percentage of questions answered correctly on the test. Finally, parents cannot assume that the child's percentile rank refers to the child's standing compared to that of other children in his class or school.

Stanines

Teachers may also use stanines to describe a student's performance on a standardized achievement test. Because the child's performance can be compared both locally and nationally using stanines, it may be the best norm to use with parents. Parents should be told that a stanine is a 9-unit scale in which a score of 5 indicates average performance. The nine stanines can be used to describe a pupil's performance, even if the parent is not clear about the reference between stanines and the normal curve. *On Telling Parents About Test Results: Test Service Notebook 154* (1980) by the Psychological Corporation, describes student performance in terms of stanines as follows:

9 Very superior
8 Superior
7 Considerably above average
6 Slightly above average
5 Average
4 Slightly below average
3 Considerably below average
2 Poor
1 Very poor (p. 4)

Some parents find this description of their child's achievement easier to understand than either the grade equivalent or the percentile rank. They can have a clear picture of whether the child is performing adequately or may need help with school work. Figure 4.6, the Individual Test Report for the *Peabody Picture Vocabulary Test-Revised* (Dunn & Dunn, 1981), shows how test scores can be reported to parents using a standard score, percentile rank, and stanine. In this example, the child achieved a percentile rank of 30 percent derived from the standard score of 92. The score placed him in the fourth stanine, or slightly below average when compared to the norm. At the primary school level, the individual pupil's test results on the *Stanford Diagnostic Reading Test* (Karlsen, Madden, & Gardner, 1976) are reported in stanines on the student's test booklet (Figure 4.7). The student, Susan, ranked in the fifth or sixth stanine on all parts of the subtest, placing her at the average or slightly above average on the test. An exception was the test on auditory vocabulary, where she ranked in the ninth or highest stanine.

REPORTING ACHIEVEMENT ON CRITERION-REFERENCED OBJECTIVES

Information on criterion-referenced objectives helps parents to see how their child is progressing on specific objectives on a standardized test. The teacher can explain how the objectives are related to the curriculum and how mastery of the objectives is determined. Parents may also be interested in knowing what plans are being made to address nonmastery items and how criterion-referenced tests

TRUE SCORE CONFIDENCE BAND

Obtained Test Scores

Raw score.........
(from page 4)

Standard score equivalent........
(from Table 1, Appendix A)

Percentile rank....
(from Table 3, Appendix A)

Stanine........
(from Table 3, Appendix A)

Age equivalent ....
(from Table 4, Appendix A)

Mark the obtained standard score equivalent on the top scale. Then draw a heavy, straight, vertical line through it, and across the three scales. This line will extend through the three obtained deviation-type test scores. Depending upon the obtained standard score, shade in a band on both sides of the vertical line, using the schedule to the right. An example is given in Figure 1.4 of the Manual.

Obtained Standard Score	AREA TO SHADE Left of line	AREA TO SHADE Right of line
Below 65	0	14
65-74	2	12
75-84	4	10
85-89	6	8
90-99	7	7

Obtained Standard Score	AREA TO SHADE Left of line	AREA TO SHADE Right of line
100-109	7	7
110-114	8	6
115-124	10	4
125-134	12	2
135 & above	14	0

This shaded area provides a confidence band: the range of scores within which the subject's true scores can be expected to fall 68 times in 100. (These band width values are based on a median standard error of measurement (SEM) of ± 7, with the band widths made increasingly asymmetrical toward the extremes to allow for *regression to the mean*.) See Part I of the Manual and the Technical Supplement for more precise values and a discussion of SEM confidence bands. Also see the Manual for a discussion of how to calculate the true score confidence band for the *age equivalent*.

Standard score scale: 40 45 50 55 60 65 70 75 80 85 90 95 100 105 110 115 120 125 130 135 140 145 150 155 160

Percentile rank scale: 1 5 10 15 20 25 30 35 40 45 50 55 60 65 70 75 80 85 90 95 99

Stanine scale: 1 2 3 4 5 6 7 8 9

EXTREMELY LOW SCORE | MODERATELY LOW SCORE | LOW / HIGH AVERAGE SCORE | MODERATELY HIGH SCORE | EXTREMELY HIGH SCORE

Data from Other Tests

Test	FORM M	Date	Results
PPVT–R			

Observations

Briefly describe the subject's test behavior, such as interest in task, quickness of response, signs of perseveration, work habits, etc.:

Performance Evaluation

This standardized test provides an *estimate* only of this individual's hearing vocabulary in Standard English, as compared with a cross-section of U.S.A. persons of the same age. Do you believe the performance of this subject represents fairly her or his true ability in this area? Yes____ No____ If not, cite reasons such as rapport problems, poor testing situation, hearing or vision loss, visual-perceptual disorder; test too easy or too hard (automatic basal or ceiling used), etc.

Recommendations

Examiner's signature

2

3

FIGURE 4.6

Peabody Picture Vocabulary Test-R: Individual Test Report

Source: Dunn and Dunn, 1981.

	TEST 2	TEST 3	TEST 1	TEST 4	TEST 5	TESTS 4 + 5
	Auditory Discrimination	Phonetic Analysis (Parts A + B)	Auditory Vocabulary	Word Reading	Reading Comprehension (Parts A + B)	Comprehension Total
Raw Score	32	34	35	33	31	64
S T A N I N E	9 8 7 6 (5) 4 3 2 1	9 8 7 6 (5) 4 3 2 1	(9) 8 7 6 5 4 3 2 1	9 8 7 (6) 5 4 3 2 1	9 8 7 6 (5) 4 3 2 1	9 8 7 6 (5) 4 3 2 1

Pupil Information Box

Name Susan

Teacher_____ Grade_____

School_____

City_____ State_____

Today's Date_____
               month   day   year

Date of Birth_____
               month   day   year

FIGURE 4.7
Stanford Diagnostic Reading Test: Primary Grade Individual Record
Source: Stanford Diagnostic Reading Test: Third Edition. Copyright © 1984 by Harcourt Brace Jovanovich, Inc. Reproduced by permission. All rights reserved.

are similar to teacher-made tests. The *Stanford Diagnostic Reading Test* results, illustrated in Figure 4.7, also exemplify how performance on specific objectives can be reported and explained to parents.

Susan was tested in the categories of Auditory Discrimination, Phonetic Analysis, Auditory Vocabulary, Word Reading, and Reading Comprehension. As her test profile reveals, she scored in the ninth stanine in auditory vocabulary, her strongest area. She was close to the mean in the remaining subtests but was weakest in auditory discrimination and reading comprehension. It is in these areas that her teacher may wish to provide additional help in order to increase her overall ability in reading.

We have considered some of the people who are associated with a child's standardized achievement test and how test results are reported to them. Although we have discussed why teachers, parents, school administrators, and school boards need information on achievement test results, we can summarize information on reporting test results by listing how each group can use the information reported.

USES OF STANDARDIZED ACHIEVEMENT TEST SCORES

School Staff

The school staff uses standardized achievement test scores for the following purposes:

> To provide information on learning achievement or progress and data for cumulative folders
> To provide a longitudinal comparison of the student's progress over a series of grades
> To provide the next teacher with one indication of the student's achievement
> To provide diagnostic information from criterion-referenced data
> To provide an evaluation of the curriculum and instruction that can be used to improve the instructional program

School Administrators

School administrators use standardized achievement test scores for the following purposes:

> To compare the school district's achievement with national norms
> To provide a record of districtwide progress in subject areas such as reading and mathematics over a school year
> To provide longitudinal information on district achievement over a period of years
> To provide an analysis of strengths and weaknesses in the curriculum and instruction within the district

Board of Education

The board of education uses standardized achievement test scores for the following purposes:

> To provide data on school achievement compared to national norms
> To provide an analysis of achievement in individual schools or programs
> To provide an analysis of instructional strengths and weaknesses in district schools

Parents

Parents use standardized achievement test scores for the following purposes:

> To understand the child's achievement compared to national norms
> To understand how the child's progress compared with the progress of other children in the same grade
> To learn the child's strengths and weaknesses on individual objectives from criterion-referenced data

SUMMARY

Information from norm-referenced and criterion-referenced tests can be very useful in evaluating achievement and considering instructional improvement. On the other hand, misuse of test results or lack of consideration of test errors and limitations can have a negative impact on instructional decisions affecting preschool and school-age children.

Despite ongoing concerns about the weaknesses of standardized tests, their use is increasing and new instruments are being developed in response to pressures for accountability for the quality of education and minimum competency standards for students and teachers.

Teachers of preschool children should be especially aware of the misuse of screening and readiness tests. With the current trend toward retaining children in kindergarten or implementing an additional preschool year for many children after kindergarten, teachers and parents need to be knowledgeable about the functions of developmental screening tests and readiness tests, as well as their limitations. The use of readiness tests results to make placement decisions about young children is of major concern, particularly when they are retained in a preschool program based on **readiness test** results.

Increasingly, early childhood educators and specialists are urging the use of a variety of methods to evaluate or test children, particularly preschool children. Standardized tests have a role, but they are only one method that should be used to evaluate young children. Informal methods, such as teacher observation and teacher-designed tasks, can also be used to obtain a more accurate picture of what preschool and primary age children have learned and achieved.

Summary Statements

1. Norm-referenced and criterion-referenced test results can be used to improve instruction for children.
2. Some standardized achievement tests are both norm referenced and criterion referenced.
3. Norm-referenced tests compare one student's performance with those of others, whereas criterion-referenced scores tell how well the student performed on specific objectives.
4. Norm-referenced tests can be used for selection purposes and to evaluate group achievement.
5. Criterion-referenced tests can be used for individual or group instructional planning.
6. Standardized test results are reported to school personnel, school boards, and parents.
7. Teachers use individual and class test records to analyze achievement and instructional needs.
8. School and district reports of standardized achievement tests are analyzed to determine the status of achievement in a school district.
9. Teachers report individual test results to parents using stanines, percentile ranks, and sometimes grade equivalents.
10. The misuse of standardized tests in early childhood programs is of major concern to some early childhood specialists and testing experts.
11. Screening tests are an efficient way to identify children who need comprehensive evaluation; however, they should not be used for diagnosis in lieu of diagnostic instruments.
12. There are difficulties with effective developmental screening because test quality varies and testing personnel may not be properly trained.
13. Many early childhood educators believe that readiness test results are misunderstood and misused with young children.
14. Some early childhood specialists recommend the use of informal measures such as observation to assess young children.

REVIEW QUESTIONS

1. How do norm-referenced and criterion-referenced tests report achievement differently?
2. Why are tests with dual referencing difficult to design?
3. Describe how test results can be used selectively.
4. How can achievement tests be used to evaluate a new instructional program?
5. Explain the purpose of a minimum-competency test.
6. What kinds of information are included on an individual test record of an achievement test?

7. What is a grade equivalent score?

8. How is a class report of an achievement test organized? What kinds of information are included?

9. Why do teachers report test results differently to different parents?

10. Explain why parents understand a stanine score more easily than a grade equivalent score.

11. Do parents find criterion-referenced scores more practical than norm-referenced scores? Why or why not?

12. Why do teachers need to understand how to interpret standardized test scores?

13. Explain why there is an increase in the use of standardized testing.

14. Do you agree with the movement for the use of minimum-competency tests? Explain your position.

15. Explain the differences between developmental screening and readiness tests.

KEY TERMS

criterion-referenced test

developmental screening

diagnostic evaluation

individualized instruction

mastery testing

minimum-competency test

norm-referenced test

readiness test

scaled score

REFERENCES

Alpern, G. D., Boll, T. J., & Shearer, M. A. (1984). *Developmental Profile II manual.* Los Angeles: Western Psychological Services.

Boehm, A. E. (1971). *Boehm Test of Basic Concepts.* New York: Psychological Corp.

California Achievement Tests: Test coordinator's handbook, Forms C and D. (1977). Monterey, CA: CTB/McGraw-Hill.

Comprehensive Tests of Basic Skills (expanded ed.) (1974). *Technical bulletin no. 1.* Monterey, CA: CTB/McGraw-Hill.

Dunn, L., & Dunn, L. (1981). *Manual Forms L and M, Peabody Picture Vocabulary Test–Revised.* Circle Pines, MN: American Guidance Service.

Durkin, D. (1987). Testing in the kindergarten. *Reading Teacher, 40,* 766–780.

Frankenburg, W. K., Dodds, J. B., Fandal, A. W., Kajuk, F., & Cohr, M. (1978). *Denver Developmental Screening Test: Revised reference manual.* Denver, CO: LADOCA Foundation.

Goodlad, J. I., Klein, M. F., & Novotny, J. M. (1973). *Early schooling in the United States.* New York: McGraw-Hill.

Goodwin, W. L., and Driscoll, L. A. (1980). *Handbook for measurement and evaluation in early childhood education.* San Francisco: Jossey-Bass.

Goodwin, W. L., and Goodwin, L. D. (1982). Measuring young children. In B. Spodek (Ed.), *Handbook of research in early childhood education.* New York: Free Press.

Gronlund, N. E. (1981). *Measurement and evaluation in teaching* (5th ed.). New York: Macmillan.

Karlsen, B., & Gardner, E. (1984). *Stanford Diagnostic Reading Test. Manual for administering and interpreting* (3rd ed.). New York: Harcourt Brace Jovanovich.

Karlsen, B., Madden, R., & Gardner, E. F. (1976). *Stanford Diagnostic Reading Test. Manual for administering and interpreting.* New York: Harcourt Brace Jovanovich.

Kaufman, A., & Kaufman, N. (1983). *Kaufman Assessment Battery for Children. Sampler manual.* Circle Pines, MN: American Guidance Service.

La Crosse, E. R., Jr. (1970). Psychologist and teacher: Cooperation or conflict? *Young Children, 25,* 223–229.

Madden, R., & Gardner, E. F. (1969, 1971). *Stanford Early Achievement Test: Directions for administering levels I and II.* New York: Harcourt Brace Jovanovich.

McCarthy, D. (1972). *Manual for the McCarthy Scales of Children's Abilities.* New York: Psychological Corp.

McCarthy, D. (1978). *McCarthy Screening Test.* New York: Psychological Corp.

Meisels, S. (1985). *Developmental screening in early childhood: A guide.* Washington, D.C.: National Association for the Education of Young Children.

Meisels, S. J. (1987). Uses and abuses of developmental screening and school readiness testing. *Young Children, 42,* 4–6, 68–73.

Meisels, S. J., & Wiske, M. S. (1983) *The early screening inventory.* New York: Teachers College Press.

National Association for the Education of Young Children. (1986). Position statement on developmentally appropriate practice in early childhood programs serving children from birth through age 8. *Young Children, 41,* 3–19.

Psychological Corp. (1984). *On telling parents about test results. Test service notebook 154.* New York: Author.

Sandford, A. R. (1974). *A manual for use of the Learning Accomplishment Profile.* Winston-Salem, NC: Kaplan School Supply.

Wechsler, D. (1967). *Wechsler Preschool and Primary Scale of Intelligence: Manual.* New York: Psychological Corp.

Wechsler, D. (1974). *Wechsler Intelligence Scale for Children–Revised: Manual.* New York: Psychological Corp.

Wilson, R. (1980). *Test Service Notebook 37: Criterion-referenced testing.* New York: Psychological Corp.

5

Informal Evaluation Measures: Observation

In the three previous chapters, we learned about standardized tests—tests that have been tried and tested with a population of test takers to establish standards for analyzing and reporting the results. We discovered how standardized tests are developed and used, their advantages and limitations, and some of the concerns of early childhood specialists concerning their use with young children.

In this chapter, we learn about informal ways of assessing and evaluating young children. These include instruments and other strategies that have been designed by teachers, other school staff members, early childhood specialists, curriculum textbook writers, and others to assess what children already know, what they have learned, and what they are prepared to learn.

TYPES OF INFORMAL EVALUATION MEASURES

Several types of informal evaluation measures are available for teachers of preschool and school-age children. These include observation, checklists and rating scales, and teacher-designed tests. In this chapter, we will discuss informal evaluation measures in general and observation strategies specifically. In the following chapters, we will examine checklists, rating scales, and teacher-designed evaluations.

Observation is a process whereby the teacher uses incidental or planned observation episodes to learn about young children. Although primary school teachers use observation techniques, particularly as part of daily instruction to evaluate their students, preschool teachers use observation as a primary method of understanding the cognitive, affective, and motor development of children throughout the school day in many instructional and play contexts.

Checklists and rating scales are teacher-developed or commercially designed lists of learning objectives for instruction in a checklist format. Checklists can be used for assessment, instructional planning, and record keeping, as well as to communicate the purposes and outcomes of the instructional program to parents and the community.

Teacher-designed evaluation measures can be written or oral tests, but can also include activities that are developmentally appropriate for young children. All of these measures are for the use of the teacher; their main purpose is to gain a better understanding of students. Regardless of the type of information acquired, the teacher's goal is to use the results to help children learn.

USES OF INFORMAL MEASURES

Standardized tests are used for two purposes: (1) to evaluate achievement compared to that of a sample group of children and (2) to measure the child's achievement on specific test objectives. The norm-referenced test measures achievement, and the criterion-referenced test evaluates mastery of test objectives. Teachers can use criterion-referenced test results to determine an individual child's strengths and weaknesses in the content areas measured by the test. Test results provide a rough idea of the child's learning needs. However, because many objectives are measured on the standardized test, there are few test questions for each objective. Consequently, criterion-referenced test results cannot be considered a completely reliable picture of the individual child's progress and instructional needs. Informal evaluation measures allow the teacher to obtain more specific information about each student's knowledge and skills relative to the instructional objectives of the class. These informal measures can be used for placement, diagnostic evaluation and instructional planning, and formative and summative evaluation.

Placement Evaluation

At the beginning of the school year and periodically during the year, preschool and primary-grade teachers must make decisions about how to place or group children. With preschool children, the teacher needs to know the skills and knowledge of each child. Because the backgrounds of the children can vary widely, the teacher will evaluate all students to determine how to plan for them in the instructional program. In preschool programs designed to prevent or deal with learning problems, the evaluation may be done to determine if the child is eligible for the program.

For school-age children, informal testing may result in placement in a group for reading and mathematics. The teacher or teams of teachers give tests at the beginning of the school year to determine the child's mastery of content objectives; their purpose is to group together children with similar learning needs for instruction. This type of evaluation may be repeated whenever teachers feel that regrouping is needed to improve instructional services for the children.

Diagnostic Evaluation and Instructional Planning

Diagnostic evaluation is more specific than placement evaluation. When assessing for diagnostic purposes, the teacher investigates the child's ability in specific objectives. With preschool children, the teacher may assign tasks involving knowledge of colors to determine which children know the colors and which ones need activities to learn them. With school-age children, the teacher may administer a paper-and-pencil test to determine which children have learned to add and which ones need to be taught that skill.

Formative and Summative Evaluation

Formative and summative evaluation occur after instruction on a particular objective or a series of objectives. **Formative evaluation** is done to determine how students are progressing toward mastery of objectives. After students practice a skill or learn information, the teacher evaluates them to determine which ones have achieved mastery and which ones need additional work, using different instructional methods or learning experiences.

   Summative evaluation is a final assessment of what children have learned. It is conducted after diagnostic and formative evaluation. For some grade levels, summative evaluation is done for grading purposes. The child receives a grade for performance on the objectives tested. Whether or not grades are used, it is hoped that children who have not mastered the information or skills tested will have more opportunities to learn.

ADVANTAGES OF USING INFORMAL EVALUATION MEASURES

Informal measures have certain advantages over standardized tests. Although they have not been validated with large numbers of students before being used in the classroom, they include measurement opportunities that standardized tests cannot provide.

   One advantage of informal measures is that they can be derived directly from the teacher's educational objectives and curriculum or from a commercial textbook curriculum. Standardized tests, by contrast, are developed to measure general objectives that are applicable to many children in different school districts and areas of the country. With informal measures, individual teachers or groups of teachers design both the curriculum and the measures to assess children's knowledge of the curriculum. Consequently, evaluation items can focus specifically on the teacher's instruction and assessment plans. Commercial publishers also can design informal means of assessment specifically for their instructional materials.

In Chapter 3 we indicated that standardized tests may not measure the way children are being taught in the classroom. Because these tests are developed over a long period of time, the test items may reflect learning objectives that are outdated. As a result, teacher-designed evaluation strategies may measure learning more accurately than standardized tests.

Valencia and Pearson (1987) argue for teacher-designed evaluation measures because research in reading instruction suggests that young readers use available resources such as text, prior knowledge, and environmental clues to make sense of reading material, whereas standardized tests evaluate reading as a set of discrete skills. As a result, these authors state, teachers teach reading as discrete skills, or teach so that students will do well on the standardized tests. Valencia and Pearson recommend that formal testing strategies be modified to better match reading research findings about effective instruction, but also that teachers use a combination of evaluation strategies that more accurately assess the reading process.

Using outdated instructional methods so that children will perform well on standardized tests can affect mathematics as well as reading. Whereas current theory of mathematics instruction stresses that children construct concepts by becoming actively involved with concrete materials, tests still measure knowledge of numerals (Kamii, 1985a, 1985b). School systems teach to the test, rather than follow methods that are best for children (National Association for the Education of Young Children, 1988).

In contrast to standardized tests, informal evaluation measures are current. Because standardized tests are developed over a period of time, there may be a lag of two or more years between test design and implementation. The test cannot be easily updated or modified. Teacher-designed evaluation measures, on the other hand, can be altered when necessary. If instructional materials are changed or learning objectives modified, the teacher can keep classroom measures current by redesigning assessment strategies to reflect the changes.

Another advantage of using informal assessment measures is that they can be correlated with diagnostic needs. If the teacher wants certain types of information for placement, grouping, and individual instructional needs, the assessment measures can be easily adapted for these purposes. Although criterion-referenced standardized tests also serve diagnostic purposes, they are generally a starting point for effective teachers. The teacher must follow criterion-referenced results with informal strategies that provide additional diagnostic information. For preschool children, who have not been given standardized tests, teacher-designed strategies are a first step in evaluation. Criterion-referenced standardized tests can be administered later when the child is more able to take them.

The flexibility of teacher-designed evaluation strategies is an important advantage. The objectives to be evaluated on a standardized test are established early in the test development process. Thereafter, objectives are not changed, and test items to measure them are evenly distributed and measure all general objectives equally. Individual teachers design both the curriculum and the measures to assess children's mastery of it; consequently, evaluation items can be tailored to the teacher's instruction and assessment plans.

DISADVANTAGES OF USING INFORMAL MEASURES

Although informal evaluation strategies have certain advantages, they also have limitations and weaknesses. Classroom teachers are more likely to use informal assessment measures than the results of standardized tests. Therefore, they must learn how to design and use informal measures appropriately if these measures are to be effective for evaluation and instructional planning. Improper development and implementation are the main disadvantages of informal measures. Specifically, problems centered on their validity and reliability, their misapplication, and their inappropriate use.

Locally designed assessment and evaluation instruments are widely used in preschools and elementary schools. Since the 1970s, when informal measures such as instructional checklists first became popular, many school districts have developed their own checklists and other assessment measures. At the preschool level, teachers and administrators have devised screening tests to determine eligibility for preschool intervention programs. For example, in some states, only children who are at risk for academic failure are eligible for state-supported kindergarten programs. Local schools are expected to determine the eligibility of the 5-year-old children in their district. The screening instruments vary greatly from one community to another.

In New York, Joiner (1977) found 151 different tests and other screening procedures being used. Only 16 of the tests were considered appropriate for screening preschool children. The Michigan Department of Education (1984) found 111 different tests being used for preschool, kindergarten, and pre–first-grade programs—and only 10 of them appropriately. Meisels (1987) stated that many locally designed screening tests have never been assessed for reliability and validity or other established criteria.

Another disadvantage of informal measures is that teachers may misuse them. Checklists are frequently used as a framework for organizing or designing the curriculum, as well as a record of evaluation of student learning. Children are tested on the checklist's objectives, and the record of their progress follows them from grade to grade. Because teachers develop their own tasks or tests to assess checklist objectives, confusion over what constitutes mastery and what kind of assessment is appropriate can cause major problems within a school or throughout a school district. In an effort to arrive at a consensus on how to assess the objectives, the strategies used by individual teachers may be severely limited. In the primary grades, teachers must frequently place a workbook page or other pencil-and-paper documentation in the child's record as proof of successful performance. This requirement eliminates the use of other informal strategies such as teacher observation or developmentally appropriate tasks for evaluation.

Durkin (1987) also observed the inappropriate use of informal evaluation measures. In the previous chapter, we discussed Durkin's reported misuse of standardized test scores for promotion and retention in preschool programs. Durkin also found that first-grade teachers used teacher-made tests and basal end-of-unit tests for grading purposes, but rarely used them to adapt instruction for students' individual learning needs.

Calfee (1987) expressed concern that curriculum, instruction, and assessment in response to external mandates are based on "a countless array of miniscule objectives" (p. 739). As a result, classroom assessment consisted of curriculum-embedded multiple-choice tests of doubtful validity.

The major disadvantage of informal measures seems to be that teachers are not prepared to develop and use them. They misuse or are unaware of the proper application of either standardized or informal measures. Some writers advocate the use of a variety of formal and informal strategies to assess young children. Teale, Hiebert, and Chittenden (1987), for example, believe that observation should be a primary tool for preschool teachers. The National Association for the Education of Young Children also strongly supports the use of observation for developmental evaluation. Its Position Statement on Developmentally Appropriate Practice in Early Childhood Programs Serving Children from Birth Through Age 8 stated the following about the developmental evaluation of children:

> Accurate testing can only be achieved with reliable, valid instruments and such instruments developed for use with young children are extremely rare. In the absence of valid instruments, testing is not valuable. Therefore, assessment of young children should rely heavily on the results of observation of their development and descriptive data. (p. 8)

Observation, like other informal strategies, requires an informed, well-prepared teacher who will use it effectively. The rest of this chapter discusses the purposes for observation and describes how observations are conducted and interpreted.

PURPOSES OF OBSERVATION

Observation is the most direct method of becoming familiar with the learning and development of the young child. Since it requires a focus on the child's behaviors, observation allows the teacher to get to know the child as a unique individual, rather than as a member of a group.

To Understand Children's Behavior

Because young children have not yet mastered language and the ability to read and write, they are unable to express themselves as clearly as older children and adults. They cannot demonstrate how much they know or understand through formal or informal measures involving tasks and standardized tests. According to child development specialists, one of the most accurate ways to learn about children is to observe them in daily activities. Because children cannot explain themselves sufficiently through language, evidence of why they behave as they do is obtained through on-the-spot recording of their actions (Irwin & Bushnell, 1980).

Children communicate through their bodies. Their physical actions reveal as much about them as the things they say. Cohen, Stern, and Balaban (1983) describe how observation of children's behavior provides information or clues to their thoughts and feelings:

> Children communicate with us through their eyes, the quality of their voices, their body postures, their gestures, their mannerisms, their smiles, their jumping up and down, their listlessness. They show us, by the way they do things as well as by what they do, what is going on inside them. When we come to see children's behavior through the eyes of its meaning to them, *from the inside out*, we shall be well on our way to understanding them. Recording their ways of communicating helps us to see them as they are. (p. 5)

To Evaluate Children's Development

A major purpose of observing children is to evaluate their development. When studying development, observation is more specific. Rather than considering behavior in general, the observer's purpose is to determine the child's progress in physical, cognitive, social, or emotional development. Observation of development not only makes it easier to understand sequences of development, but also helps teachers of young children to be aware of individual growth and aids children who have delays in specific areas of development.

Beaty (1986) describes observation of development as systematic. There are specific purposes for observing and particular methods for collecting and recording observation data. Beaty proposes eight reasons for systematically observing and recording the development of young children:

1. To make an initial assessment of the child's abilities.
2. To determine a child's areas of strength and areas needing strengthening.
3. To make individual plans based on observed needs.
4. To conduct an ongoing check on the child's progress.
5. To learn more about child development in particular areas.
6. To resolve a particular problem involving the child.
7. To use in reporting to parents, or specialists in health, speech, mental health.
8. To gather information for the child's folder, for use in guidance and placement.
   (p. 5)

Because what is observed must be interpreted, the observer must know how to use observation to gather specific data. Background information on how children develop and learn is important if the observer is to be able to convert the child's behaviors into information that can be used to understand the child's level of development and the need for experiences that will further that development.

Obviously, the quality of the information gained from an observation depends on the skills of the observer. The sophisticated observer uses knowledge of developmental theories, and of stages of development, to note the significant events of an observation and to interpret those events in a way that is useful in understanding the child. For example, a teacher may notice that a child is exploring or playing with a collection of buttons in making a pile of all the buttons with four holes. A knowledge of Piaget's cognitive developmental theory will enable the teacher to interpret this activity as the ability to classify objects.

Bentzen (1985) states that observation is not simply looking at something; it is a disciplined, scientific process of searching for a behavior in a particular way. The observer must know what to look for, how to record the desired information, and how to explain the behavior.

Young children develop rapidly, and their level of development changes continually. By observing frequently, teachers can track the child's development, and respond to changes and advances in development, with new opportunities and challenges.

TYPES OF OBSERVATION

What happens during an observation? What does the observer actually do? When conducting an observation, the student, teacher, or researcher visits a classroom or other place where a group of children may be observed as they engage in routine activities. The observer, having already determined the objectives or purpose of the observation, the time to be spent studying the child or children, and the form in which the observation will be conducted and recorded, sits at the side or in an observation booth and watches the children. The types of observation used include anecdotal records, running records, speciman records, time sampling, event sampling, and checklists and rating scales.

Anecdotal Record

An **anecdotal record** is a written description of a child's behavior. It is an objective account of an incident that tells what happened, when, and where. The record may be used to understand some aspect of behavior. Anecdotal records may be used to track the development of an infant or young child by a physician, parents, or teachers to explain unusual behavior. Although the narrative itself is objective, comments may be added as an explanation of or reaction to the recorded incident.

There are five characteristics of the anecdotal record (Goodwin and Driscoll, 1980):

1. The anecdotal record is the result of direct observation.
2. The anecdotal record is a prompt, accurate, and specific account of an event.

3. The anecdotal record includes the context of the behavior.
4. Interpretations of the incident are recorded separately from the incident.
5. The anecdotal record focuses on behavior that is either typical or unusual for the child being observed.

Figure 5.1 is an example of the form and content of an anecdotal record.

Running Record

The **running record** is another method of recording behavior. It is a more detailed narrative of a child's behavior that includes the sequence of events. The running record includes everything that occurred over a period of time—that is, all behavior observed rather than particular incidents that are used for the anecdotal record. The description is objective. An effort is made to record everything that happened or was said during the observation period. Running records may be recorded over a period ranging from a few minutes to a few weeks or even months.

Child Name(s): <u>Robbie, Mary Josie</u>
Age: <u>4</u>
Location: <u>Sunnyside Preschool</u>
Observer: <u>Sue</u>
Type of Development Observed: <u>Social/Emotional</u>

Incident	Social/Emotional Notes or Comments
Mary and Josie were in the Housekeeping Area pretending to fix a meal. Robbie came to the center and said he wanted to eat. The girls looked at him. Janie said, "You can't play here, we're busy." Ron stood watching the girls as they moved plastic fruit on the table. Robbie said, "I could be the Daddy and do the dishes." Mary thought for a minute, looked at Janie, and replied, "Oh, all right, you can play."	The girls play together frequently and tend to discourage others from entering their play. Robbie has learned how to enter a play group. He was careful not to upset the girls. They relented when he offered to be helpful. Robbie is usually successful in being accepted into play activities.

FIGURE 5.1
Example of an anecdotal record

The observer comments on or analyzes the behaviors separately after studying the record. Her task is to record the situation so that future readers can visualize what occurred (Cohen, Stern, & Balaban, 1983). Figure 5.2, pp. 94–95, is an example of a running record.

Specimen Record

Specimen records are very similar to running records. They are even more detailed and precise. Beaty (1986) defined running records as an informal method used by teachers. Specimen records, in contrast, are used by researchers who are not part of classroom activities and are removed from the children. Researchers may later code observation information to analyze the findings. For example, specimen records were used in a study of child care settings in Chicago. As part of the study, observation was used to determine caregiver behaviors. Researchers coded each utterance by a caregiver to a child, as well as every incident of playing, helping, teaching, touching, kissing, and hitting (Clark-Stewart, 1987).

Time Sampling

The purpose of **time sampling** is to record the frequency of a behavior for a designated period of time. The observer decides ahead of time what behaviors will be observed, what the time interval will be, and how the behaviors will be recorded. The observer observes these behaviors and records how many times they occur during preset, uniform time periods. Other behaviors that occur during the observation are ignored. After a number of samplings have been completed, the data are studied to determine when and perhaps why a behavior is occurring. The observer can use the information to help the child if a change in behavior is desired.

Time sampling may be used with young children because many of their behaviors are brief. By using time sampling, the observer can gain more comprehensive information about the behavior. The length of the observation can be affected by the target behavior, the children's familiarity with the observer, the nature of the situation, and the number of children to be observed (Webb, Campbell, Schwartz, & Sechrest, 1966).

Time sampling is frequently used by teachers or other school staff members when a child is behaving inappropriately at school—for example, one who behaves aggressively with other children and does not cooperate in classroom routines at certain times. It is used over a period of time during the hours of the daily schedule when the unwanted behavior occurs. After the time samples are studied, the teacher can determine what can be done to modify the behavior. Figure 5.3, p. 96, demonstrates the use of time sampling as an observation method.

Event Sampling

Event sampling is used instead of time sampling when a behavior tends to occur in a particular setting rather than during a predictable time period. The behavior may occur at odd times or infrequently; event sampling is commonly used to discover its causes or results. The observer determines when the behavior is likely to occur and waits for it to take place. The drawback of this method is that if the event does not occur readily, the observer's time will be wasted.

Because event sampling is a cause-and-effect type of observation, the teacher or observer is looking for clues that will assist in solving the child's problem. Bell and Low (1973) used *ABC analysis* with the observed incident to understand the cause of the behavior. *A* is the antecedent event, *B* is the target behavior, and *C* is the consequent event. Using ABC analysis with event sampling permits the observer to learn how to address the problem with the child. Figure 5.4, p. 97, is an example of event sampling with ABC analysis to interpret the incident, and Figure 5.5 is an observation form that is adaptable to various types of observations.

Checklists and Rating Scales

Although a whole chapter (6) is devoted to checklists and rating scales, it is useful to include them in this discussion of observation techniques. **Checklists** are lists of sequential behaviors arranged in a system of categories. The observer can use the checklist to determine if the child exhibits the behaviors or skills listed. The checklist is useful when many behaviors are to be observed. It can also be used fairly quickly and easily.

The **rating scale,** on the other hand, provides a means to determine the degree to which the child exhibits a behavior or the quality of that behavior. Each trait is rated on a continuum, allowing the observer to decide where the child fits on the scale. Rating scales are helpful when the teacher needs to evaluate a wide range of behaviors at one time.

OBSERVING DEVELOPMENT

We mentioned earlier that young children develop rapidly. At this time, we need to consider the meaning of development in more detail. Development is continuous, sequential, and involves change over time.

Development can be defined in part as the process of change in an individual over time. As the individual ages, certain changes take place. Development is thus affected by the child's chronological age, rate of maturation, and individual experiences. Children of the same chronological age are not necessarily in the same stage or level of development, possibly because they mature at different rates and have different experiences and opportunities. The child who has many opportunities to climb, run, and jump in outdoor play may demonstrate advanced motor development skills compared with the child who spends most play periods indoors.

Developmental change can be both quantitative and qualitative. Physical growth is quantitative and cumulative. New physical skills are added to those already present. Developmental change can also be qualitative. When changes in psychological characteristics such as speech, emotions, or intelligence occur, development is reorganized at a higher level.

Observation	Notes or Comments

Child's Name: <u>Christopher</u>
Age: <u>4</u>
Location: <u>KinderKare</u>
Date and Time: <u>June 21, 1988</u>   <u>8:40–9:10</u>
Observer: <u>Cindy</u>
Type of Development Observed: <u>Social and Cognitive</u>

Observation	Notes or Comments
Chris is playing with a toy. He says, "Kelly, can I keep it?" several times until he gets an answer. He moves on to a toy guitar and plays it while he supervises the other children by walking around the room. He tells everyone to sit down at the tables after the teacher says to.	Chris is polite to others. Chris is helping his classmates to follow the rules.
Chris sits by a friend and talks about eating granola bars. He watches and listens to the conversation on either side of him. He's still unaffected by the loud temper tantrum of another child. Then he notices her and watches. He tries to explain this behavior to the others by saying a plant was split.	Chris is interested in what others have to say. Chris tries to make sense of a child's behavior.
He follows teacher's directions. Then he decides he wants to be in on a secret. A boy shoves him away. Chris informs him that he *can* hear if he wants to. This has caused him to disobey the teacher. He has to sit out of the circle. He walks over to the chair, sits down, gets up immediately, comes back to the circle undetected by the teacher. He joins the circle.	Chris chooses appropriate ways to assert himself.

FIGURE 5.2
Example of a running record

Observation	Notes or Comments
Chris tattles on a child hiding money. He is told to switch places and wants to know why. He gets up to push the chairs under the table without being asked directly. He wants to explain the temper tantrum to another child (it is still going on) who is curious.	Chris needs to know why he does some things.
Chris attends to the teacher's questions and the story that she is now reading. He begins to look around the circle and then back to the book. He plays with his socks and participates in the group answers to questions about the story. (*Now One Foot, Now the Other Foot* by Tomie dePaola (he is in continuous motion with some part of his body during the story). Now he becomes very still and attends to the story. He puts both hands over his ears when students remark about events in the story. He immediately makes his own remarks. He becomes very still again. The whole circle is quiet for the ending of the book.	Chris shows he has self-control. Chris responds to and sympathizes with the characters in the story.
As soon as the story is finished, Chris says, "I got a cut from a thorn bush." He sits quietly but moves around. "How do we kill our plants over there?" he asks the teacher. (A plant was knocked off earlier.) "Not mine, not me!" he says.	

FIGURE 5.2
(continued)

Child's Name(s): Joanie		
Age: 5		
Location: Rosewood School Kindergarten		
Date and Time: May 17, 10:45–11:00		
Observer: Nancy		
Type of Development Observed: Joanie Has Difficulty Completing Tasks		

Event	Time	Notes or Comments
Art Center—leaves coloring activity on table unfinished	10:45	Some of Joanie's behaviors seem to be resulting from failure to follow procedures for use of materials.
Library—looks at book, returns it to shelf.	10:50	Behavior with the puzzles may come from frustration.
Manipulative Center—gets frustrated with puzzle, piles pieces in center—leaves on table. Pulls out	10:55	
Lego blocks, starts to play. When teacher signals to put toys away, Joanie leaves Lego blocks on table and joins other children.	11:00	Joanie may need help in putting away with verbal rewards for finishing a task and putting materials away.
		Encourage Joanie to get help with materials that are too hard.

FIGURE 5.3
Example of time sampling

Development is also characterized as continuous. The individual is constantly changing. In quantitative change, the individual is continually adding new skills or abilities. In qualitative change, the individual is incorporating new development with existing characteristics to create more sophisticated psychological traits.

Finally, development is sequential. Each individual develops at a different rate; however, the sequence or pattern of development is the same. All children move through stages of development in the same sequence, whose characteristics are described by Bentzen (1985) as follows:

1. Stages or steps in development do not vary. Children do not skip a stage of development.

2. Children progress through the stages in the same order.
3. All children, regardless of cultural or social differences, progress through the stages in the same order. The stages are universal. (p. 21)

Physical Development

Preschool children are in the most important period of physical and motor development. Beginning with babies, who are in the initial stages of learning to control their bodies, physical development is rapid and continues into the primary school years.

Observations of physical development focus on both types of motor development: gross and fine. Gross motor skills refer to the movements and abilities of the large muscles of the body in physical activities such as walking, running, climbing, swinging, jumping, and throwing. Preschool children are in a period of mastering large motor skills. At play, they use play equipment and other activities to practice motor skills.

Fine motor skills involve the body's small muscles—specifically, the hands and fingers. These skills are used for eating, dressing, writing, using small con-

---

Child's Name(s): Helen
Age: 4
Location: May's Child Enrichment Center
Date and Time: 2/4   2:30–3:30
Observer: Marcy
Type of Development Observed: Social/Emotional
    Helen uses frequent hitting behavior

Time	Antecedent Event	Behavior	Consequent Event
2:41	Helen and Rosie are eating a snack. Rosie takes part of Helen's cracker.	Helen hits Rosie.	Rosie calls to the teacher.
3:20	John is looking at a book in the Library Center. Helen asks for the book. John refuses.	Helen grabs the book and hits John.	John hits back and takes back the book. Helen gets another book and sits down.

FIGURE 5.4
Example of event sampling

Name _____
Date _____
Time _____
Location _____
Child(ren) Observed _____
_____
Age _____
Type of Development Observed: _____
Type of Observation Used: _____

Purposes of Observation:

1.

2.

3.

Questions Answered:

1.

2.

3.

Description of Observation (Anecdotal, Time Sampling, Running Record,
    Event Sampling):

Summary of Important Behaviors Recorded and Comments

FIGURE 5.5
Sample observation form

struction toys, and performing many tasks. They evolve after gross motor skills have been mastered.

Purposes of Observing Physical Development
Physical development is observed for the following reasons:

1. To learn how children develop gross and fine motor skills
2. To become familiar with the kinds of physical activities young children engage in as they practice the use of gross and fine motor skills
3. To become familiar with individual differences in physical development

Questions Answered by Observation of Physical Development
Physical development is observed to answer the following questions:

1. What are the child's physical characteristics? How do these characteristics affect the child's motor abilities?
2. What types of large motor activities does the child enjoy? What kinds of activities does the child use to exercise and develop gross motor skills?
3. What types of small motor activities does the child enjoy? What kinds of activities does the child use to develop and exercise fine motor skills?

Social and Emotional Development

Social and emotional development are also significant areas of development during the preschool years. In this period, the child moves from egocentricity to social interaction with others. When a child is able to use social behaviors, he influences others and is influenced by them. As children interact in various contexts, they are able to develop and expand their repertoire of social skills.

Emotional development parallels and affects social development. The preschool child refines behaviors as he experiences emotions such as happiness, anger, joy, jealousy, and fear. According to Bentzen (1985), the most common emotions in preschool children are aggression, dependency, and fear. Aggression is a behavior that is intended to hurt another person or property. Dependency causes behaviors such as clinging, seeking approval, assistance, reassurance, and demands for attention. Fearfulness includes behaviors such as crying and avoiding the feared situation.

Purposes of Observing Social and Emotional Development
Social and emotional development is observed for the following reasons:

1. To learn how children develop social skills
2. To become familiar with how children learn about social interactions
3. To understand how children differ in social skill development
4. To become familiar with the ways preschool children handle their emotions
5. To be aware of differences in children's emotional behaviors and responses

**Questions Answered by Observations of Social
and Emotional Development**
Social and emotional development is observed to answer the following questions:

1. How do children demonstrate social awareness and prosocial skills?
2. How do children develop leadership skills? What behaviors make it easier to assume a leadership role?
3. How do children use different prosocial styles? How do they develop successful prosocial skills?
4. How does the child resolve conflicts? How is the behavior representative of the child's social and emotional development?
5. How does the child use and handle aggressive behaviors?
6. What kinds of events trigger dependence or fear?
7. What kinds of behaviors demonstrate the interdependence of social and emotional development?

Cognitive Development

Cognitive development, which stems from mental functioning, is concerned with how the child learns about and understands the world. Cognitive abilities develop as the child interacts with the environment. Our descriptions of cognitive development are derived largely from Piaget's theory of development.

Piaget described cognitive development in terms of stages. The quality of the child's thinking progresses as the child moves through the stages. The infant is in the sensorimotor stage, which lasts until about 18 months of age. During this stage, intellectual growth occurs through the senses and innate reflexive actions. In the latter part of the sensorimotor stage, symbolic thought develops that is characterized by improved memory.

Between the ages of 2 and 6 years, the child moves through the preoperations stage. In this stage, the ability to use language is developed. The child is egocentric, unable to view another person's perspective. Thinking is bounded by perception. Later, when the child reaches the stage of concrete operations, he is able to move beyond perceptual thinking. Cognitive abilities become qualitatively different. The child is now able to grasp concepts such as classification, seriation, one-to-one correspondence, and causality because he has attained conservation (Morrison, 1988).

The child's use of mental processes to understand knowledge develops gradually, and cognitive abilities evolve over a long period of time. Piaget attributed cognitive development to maturity, experiences, and social transmission. Therefore, the child's family, environment, and opportunities for experiences affect the development of cognitive abilities. Knowledge is reconstructed as the child organizes and restructures experiences to refine and expand his own understanding.

Purposes of Observing Cognitive Development

Cognitive development is observed for the following reasons:

1. To understand how children use their cognitive abilities to learn
2. To understand the differences in children's cognitive styles
3. To become familiar with how children develop the ability to use classification, seriation, and one-to-one correspondence
4. To understand how the child uses play and interaction with materials to extend his cognitive abilities
5. To become familiar with how children think and what they are capable of learning
6. To evaluate what children have learned

Questions Answered by Observation of Cognitive Development

Cognitive development is observed to answer the following questions:

1. How is the child's learning affected by his cognitive abilities?
2. How does the child use emerging cognitive abilities (conservation, one-to-one correspondence, seriation) naturally in classroom experiences?
3. How do children differ in cognitive development and cognitive characteristics?
4. How do classroom experiences affect the opportunities for cognitive development?
5. How is the child's cognitive knowledge demonstrated nonverbally?
6. What behaviors does the child exhibit to indicate that learning has occurred following classroom experiences and instruction?

Language Development

The acquisition of language is one of the major accomplishments of children during the preschool and primary-grade years. During the first 8 years of life, the child rapidly acquires vocabulary, grammar, and syntax. As in other types of development, the child's use of language changes, increases, and is refined over a period of time.

While babies begin using speech as single utterances, toddlers and preschoolers expand their repertoire into two words, three words, and increasingly complex statements. As the child's ability to use language expands to include questions and other grammatical elements, the child uses trial and error to approximate more closely the syntax and grammar of adult speech.

Language development is also related to cognitive development. When the child's thinking is egocentric, his language reflects this pattern. The egocentric child talks to himself and does not use language to communicate with other children. The child who is shedding egocentric thinking uses socialized speech to communicate with others. He not only shares conversations with peers and adults, but listens and responds to what others are saying.

Purposes of Observing Language Development
Language development is observed for the following reasons:

1. To become aware of the child's ability to use language to communicate
2. To understand the difference between egocentric and socialized speech
3. To learn how the child uses syntax, grammar, and vocabulary in the process of expanding and refining his language
4. To become aware of differences in language development among individual children

Questions Answered by Observation of Language Development
Language development is observed to answer the following questions:

1. How does the child use language to practice using speech?
2. When do children tend to use egocentric speech? Socialized speech?
3. How does the extent of vocabulary vary among children?
4. What can be observed about the child's use of sentence structure?
5. How can errors in the use of language reveal the child's progress in refining language?

ADVANTAGES AND DISADVANTAGES OF USING OBSERVATION FOR EVALUATION

Observation is a valuable evaluation tool. Teachers can use it to gather the kind of information that may not be available from structured methods of measurement.

When observed, children are engaged in daily activities that are a natural part of the classroom routine. The observer is able to see the typical ways children respond to learning tasks, play activities, and individual and group lessons. The observer can notice the child's behaviors and the background factors that influence the behaviors.

Learning can also be evaluated by observation. The teacher can observe the child's responses in a group during a lesson, or while the child engages in exploration with construction materials. Areas of development such as gross motor skills can be observed on the playground; language skills can be noted by listening to the language of two children in the art center.

An advantage of observation is that the observer can focus on the behavior or information that is needed. If a child is exhibiting aggression, the observer can focus on aggressive incidents to help the child use more appropriate behaviors in interactions with other children. If a child is beginning to use prosocial skills more effectively, the teacher can observe group interactions and encourage the child to continue to improve.

However, although observation allows one to concentrate on specific behaviors, it can also cause difficulties. The observer can miss details that make a significant difference in the quality of the data gathered. Because many incidents and behaviors may occur during the observation, there is the danger that the observer may focus on the wrong behaviors. Or the observer may become less attentive during the observation period, resulting in variations in the information obtained (Webb, Campbell, Schwartz, & Sechrest, 1966).

Observer bias is another disadvantage. If the observer has preconceived notions about how the child behaves or performs, these ideas can affect the observer's interpretation of the information obtained from watching the child.

Observations can be misleading when the incident observed is taken out of context. Although an observed behavior is often brief, it must be understood in context. A frequent mistake of inexperienced observers is to interpret a single incident as a common occurrence. For example, the observer who witnesses a teacher losing patience with a child may interpret the incident as that teacher's normal behavior. In reality, however, this behavior may be rare. The presence of the observer can also affect children's behavior. Because children are aware that they are being watched, their behaviors may not be typical. As a result, the validity of the observation may be doubtful (Webb, Campbell, Schwartz, & Sechrest, 1966).

OBSERVATION GUIDELINES

For college students and others who have not previously conducted observations, certain guidelines will now be presented. The observer who is seeking a site for observation needs to know how to go about finding a school or early childhood center and how to observe effectively once it has been selected.

Determining the Observation Site

The observation site depends on the type of observation to be done. First, the observer wants to know that children at the school or early childhood center engage in the activities of interest to the observer. For example, if the observer wishes to see activities that are typical of a Montessori classroom, it would be wise to find out if these activities will be taking place during the observation period. Once the purpose of the observation has been determined, the observer must decide on an optimum location. If the objective is to learn about creativity in the young child, it is frustrating to spend time in a program where art experiences are limited or infrequent. Likewise, if the purpose is to observe behaviors in a child-centered environment, it would be inappropriate to visit a structured program directed by the teacher.

Once the center or school has been selected, the observer should contact it ahead of time. Although many settings welcome observers on a walk-in basis, most early childhood programs request or require advance notification. Some settings do not allow observers or schedule them in ways designed to protect children from interruptions. Some schools allow observations on certain days. Others wish to be contacted well in advance because many people wish to observe their program. Many child care centers schedule field trips frequently and wish to avoid inconveniencing their observers. Whatever the reason, it is best to contact the observation site before scheduling the observation.

Observer Behaviors During the Observation Visit

The observer is a guest of the center or school. Although the opportunity to study the children is important, it is also important to avoid disrupting activities in progress. The observer may want to share the purpose of the observation with staff members or the teacher in the classroom being visited. In addition, the observer should conduct the observation in a manner that is compatible with the teacher's style of leadership in the type of program being observed. For example, Montessori schools frequently restrict visitors to certain areas of the classroom and may discourage any interaction with the children. Another school or program may encourage the observer to talk to the children or take part in their activities.

In most cases, the observer should be unobtrusive. Because children are sensitive to the presence of visitors and may alter their behaviors when a stranger is in the room, observers can minimize such changes by drawing as little attention to their presence as possible. Observers may seat themselves in a position that does not draw the children's attention. Sometimes it is helpful to avoid looking at the children for a few minutes until they become acclimated. Postponing the writing of observation notes for a few minutes may also help to prevent disruption.

Dress can make a difference. Observers who are dressed in simple clothing of one color rather than bright garments with bold patterns are less likely to draw undue attention to their presence. Dress should also be appropriate. Clothing that is too casual may be offensive to the adults in the early childhood center. Observers should err on the side of being dressed too formally rather than in an unprofessional manner (Irwin & Bushnell, 1980).

Ethics During the Observation Visit

Observers must be alert to the proper way to use the information gathered during an observation. The privacy of the children, their family, and school staff members must be considered. When individual children are observed, only the child's first name should be used. Information from any observation should be considered confidential and safeguarded from casual perusal by others. The child should not be discussed in an unprofessional manner with other observers, school staff members, or outsiders.

Avoiding Personal Bias

Personal bias can affect the observer's reaction to and report of an observation. If observers are aware of how their background and previous experiences can influence their report, they can avoid using personal opinion when analyzing the data collected during an observation.

One cause of observer bias is differences in value systems. It is easy to apply one's own value system when observing in a school. For example, a middle-class observer may misunderstand the nature of aggression exhibited by young children in an inner-city ghetto. It is also possible to impose personal values on the language of a child from a home where cursing is a common form of communication. The observer needs to be aware of such possible biases and avoid them when interpreting observational information.

The observer's reaction to the site can also distort her use of observational data. Each observer has a perception of the characteristics of a "good" school or center. When observing an early childhood program that does not fit this definition, the observer may impose a negative interpretation on the information gathered. The reaction to the setting affects how the observer perceives the behaviors observed.

An observation can also be biased by the time of the observation or the briefness of the visit. Observers frequently react to a teacher's behavior and conclude that the teacher always engages in practices that the observer considers inappropriate. Observers need to understand that what they see during a short visit may give them an incomplete, distorted perception of the teacher or setting. The observer would have to make many visits during different times of the day over a long period of time before being able to draw conclusions about the quality of teaching or the environment. One or two brief observations provide only a small glimpse of the nature of the teacher and the classroom visited.

SUMMARY

Although standardized tests are used to evaluate children's learning, informal strategies are also essential, particularly for use by classroom teachers. They provide a variety of evaluation methods by which teachers acquire comprehensive information about their students' development and learning.

Informal evaluation methods include checklists and rating scales, teacher-designed activities and written tests, and observation. Each type of evaluation gives the teacher flexibility and variability in acquiring information needed to assess children's learning and development and to plan instruction to meet the needs of each student.

Observation is used to assess learning and to gather information regarding children's development. Because young children cannot demonstrate knowledge in a written test, teachers of preschool children use observation to learn about children's development, as well as about the knowledge they have acquired.

There are several types of observation, each with a specific purpose. Observers can use anecdotal records, running records, time sampling, event sampling, and checklists and rating scales to gather information about young children.

Summary Statements

1. Besides formal or standardized tests, informal measures can be used for evaluation.
2. Informal evaluation measures can be more useful to classroom teachers than standardized test results.
3. Informal evaluation measures include observation, checklists and rating scales, and teacher-designed assessments.
4. Informal evaluation measures can be used for placement, diagnosis, instructional planning, and assessment of learning.
5. Informal evaluation measures are advantageous for teachers because they can be closely correlated with the teacher's curriculum and changed when instruction is modified.
6. Some researchers prefer teacher-designed evaluation strategies because they are more appropriate for recent instructional trends.
7. Informal measures may lack validity and reliability or may be misused by teachers and administrators.
8. Observation is a useful way for preschool teachers to learn about children's development and to understand their behavior.
9. Observation of young children is essential because they cannot communicate verbally what they are thinking, feeling, and understanding.
10. There are many observation techniques that allow observers to gather information.
11. Information about young children's physical, social, emotional, cognitive, and language development can be acquired through observation of normal daily activities in the classroom.
12. Although observation has obvious advantages as an evaluation tool, if used incorrectly, it can result in incomplete or inaccurate information about children.

REVIEW QUESTIONS

1. Why is it important to use informal evaluation methods, particularly with preschool and primary school children?
2. Explain how different types of informal evaluation provide unique kinds of information about young children.
3. How do the purposes of informal evaluation differ from the purposes of standardized testing?
4. Describe some ways that teachers can use informal evaluation measures for instructional planning.
5. What is diagnostic evaluation?
6. What are the differences between formative and summative evaluation?

7. Why do informal evaluation measures produce immediate results compared with standardized test results?

8. How are informal measures misused in elementary schools?

9. How are teachers unaware of the proper use of formal and informal evaluation measures?

10. Describe some purposes of using observation techniques with preschool and school-age children.

11. Why is observation of development systematic and specific?

12. Explain the purposes of the different types of observation: (a) anecdotal records, (b) running records, (c) specimen records, (d) time sampling, (e) event sampling, and (f) checklists and rating scales. What is unique about specimen records?

13. How are other types of development related to the child's cognitive development?

14. How does egocentrism affect cognitive, social, and language development?

15. How can the observer's experience and skills affect the quality of the information gained from observing young children?

KEY TERMS

anecdotal record

checklist

event sampling

formative evaluation

rating scale

running record

specimen record

summative evaluation

time sampling

REFERENCES

Beaty, J. J. (1986). *Observing development of the young child*. Columbus, OH: Charles E. Merrill.

Bell, D., & Low, R. M. (1977). *Observing and recording children's behavior*. Richland, WA: Performance Associates.

Bentzen, W. R. (1985). *Seeing young children: A guide to observing and recording behavior*. Albany, NY: Delmar.

Calfee, R. C. (1987). The school as a context for assessment of literacy. *The Reading Teacher*, 40, 738–743.

Clark-Stewart, A. (1987). Predicting child development from child care forms and features: The Chicago study. In D. A. Phillips (Ed.), *Quality in child care: What does research tell us?* (pp. 21–41). Washington, D.C.: National Association for the Education of Young Children.

Cohen, D. H., Stern, V., & Balaban, N. (1983). *Observing and recording the behavior of young children.* New York: Teachers College Press.

Durkin, D. (1987). Testing in the kindergarten. *The Reading Teacher, 40,* 766–770.

Goodwin, W. R., & Driscoll, L. A. (1980). *Handbook for measurement and evaluation in early childhood education.* San Francisco: Jossey-Bass.

Irwin, D. M., & Bushnell, M. M. (1980). *Observational strategies for child study.* New York: Holt, Rinehart, & Winston.

Joiner, L. M. (1977). A technical analysis of the variation in screening instruments and programs in New York State. ERIC: ED 154 596.

Kamii, C. (1985a). Leading primary education toward excellence: Beyond worksheets and drill. *Young Children, 40,* 3–9.

Kamii, C. (1985b). *Young children reinvent arithmetic.* New York: Teachers College Press.

Meisels, S. J. (1987). Uses and abuses of developmental screening and school readiness testing. *Young Children, 42,* 4–6, 68–73.

Michigan Department of Education. (1984). *Superintendent's study group on early childhood education.* Lansing, MI: Author.

Morrison, G. (1988). *Education and development of infants, toddlers, and preschoolers.* Glenview, IL: Scott, Foresman.

National Association for the Education of Young Children. (1986). Position statement on developmentally appropriate practice in early childhood programs serving children from birth through age 8. *Young Children, 41,* 3–19.

National Association for the Education of Young Children. (1988). Position statement on standardized testing of young children 3 through 8 years of age. *Young Children, 43,* 42–47.

Teale, W. H., Hiebert, E. H., & Chittenden, E. A. (1987). Assessing young children's literacy development. *The Reading Teacher, 40,* 772–777.

Valencia, S., & Pearson, P. D. (1987). Reading assessment: Time for a change. *The Reading Teacher, 40,* 726–732.

Webb, E. J., Campbell, D. T., Schwartz, R. D., & Sechrest, L. (1966). *Unobtrusive measures.* Chicago: Rand McNally.

6
Informal Evaluation Measures: Checklists and Rating Scales

I n Chapter 5, we introduced the topic of informal measurement instruments and strategies. The purposes of informal measures were discussed, as well as their strengths and weaknesses. One informal evaluation strategy, observation, was described in detail. In this chapter, we will learn about another type of evaluation strategy that involves the use of teacher-designed instruments: *checklists* and *rating scales*. Because checklists are used more extensively than rating scales by early childhood and primary school teachers, we will discuss them first. A description of rating scales will follow so that the reader can understand how they are designed and used, and how they differ from checklists.

CHECKLISTS
Purposes of Checklists

Checklists are made from a collection of learning objectives or indicators of development. The lists of items are arranged to give the user an overview of their sequence and of how they relate to each other. The lists of items are then organized into a checklist format so that the teacher can use them for various purposes in the instructional program. Because the checklists are representative of the curriculum for the grade level, they become a framework for assessment and evaluation, instructional planning, record keeping, and communicating with parents about what is being taught and how their child is progressing.

Using Checklists with Preschool Children

Children in the years from birth to age 8 move rapidly through different stages of development. Doctors, psychologists, parents, and developmental specialists want to understand and monitor the development of individual children and groups of children. The developmental indicators for children at different stages and ages have been established; lists and checklists of these indicators can be used to monitor development. When evaluating a child's development, many types of professionals use a **developmental checklist** format to evaluate development and record the results.

Preschool teachers use checklists to evaluate and record developmental progress. The individual child's developmental progress provides important clues to the kinds of experiences she needs and can enjoy. For instance, the teacher keeps track of the child's use of fine motor skills. When the child is able to use the fingers to grasp small objects, cutting activities may be introduced. In language development, the teacher can evaluate the child's speaking vocabulary and use of syntax, and thus choose the best stories to read to the child.

Teachers often use checklists to screen children who enter preschool programs or to select them for programs. Developmental or cognitive tasks are used to identify children with special needs. Because these checklists include behaviors that are characteristic of a stage of development, children who do not exhibit these behaviors can be referred for additional screening and testing (Morrison, 1988).

Checklists are also used to design learning experiences at the preschool level. The teacher surveys the list of learning objectives that are appropriate for that age group of children and uses the list to plan learning activities in the classroom. These checklists can also be used to assess the child's progress in learning the objectives and to keep records of progress and further instructional needs. When talking to parents about the instructional program, the teacher can discuss what is being taught and how their child is benefiting from the learning experiences.

Using Checklists with School-Age Children

The use of checklists for primary school children is very similar to their use with preschool children. In fact, curriculum checklists can be a continuation of those used in the preschool grades. However, there are two differences. First, fewer developmental characteristics are recorded, and cognitive or academic objectives become more important. Second, school-age checklists become more differentiated in areas of learning. Whereas teachers are concerned with motor development, language development, social and emotional development, and cognitive development at the preschool level, at the primary level, curriculum content areas become more important. Thus, with primary-grade checklists, objectives are more likely to be organized in terms of mathematics, language arts, science, social studies, and physical education.

Diagnosis of learning strengths and weaknesses in curriculum objectives becomes more important in the primary grades, and assessment of progress in learning may become more precise and segmented. Checklist objectives may appear on report cards as the format for reporting achievement to parents. Likewise, the checklist items may be representative of achievement test objectives, state-mandated objectives, textbook objectives, and locally selected objectives. Figure 6.1 shows how the Essential Elements used in the state of Texas have been incorporated in a checklist format for reporting to parents.

HOW CHECKLISTS ARE DESIGNED AND USED

Checklists of development and instructional objectives have been used in education for several decades. When educators and early childhood specialists worked with Head Start and other programs aimed at improving education for special populations of students, they developed outlines of educational objectives to describe the framework of learning that children should experience. Since that time, checklists have been further developed and used at all levels of education. Reading series designed for elementary grades include a scope and sequence of skills, and many school districts have a list of objectives for every course or grade level. Figure 6.2 shows a typical checklist developed by a school district for mathematics at the elementary level. The Texas Education Agency has developed a sequence of objectives for all school districts in the state to follow called *Essential Elements*. The Essential Elements range from preschool programs for 4-year-old children to all content areas at the secondary level. The Essential Elements (Texas Education Agency, 1985) for science in kindergarten are described as follows:

> (a) *Science, kindergarten shall have a balance of content and activities from the life, earth, and physical sciences and shall include the following essential elements:*
> (1) Manipulative laboratory skills. The student shall be provided opportunities to:
>   (A) use comparators: color, texture, taste, odor, size, shape, direction, motion, heat/cold, sink/float, sound; and
>   (B) practice safety
> (2) The use of skills in acquiring data through the senses. The student shall be provided opportunities to:
>   (A) observe color, texture, size, shape of objects;
>   (B) observe objects in the environment; and
>   (C) observe events and changes in the environment
> (3) The use of classification skills in ordering and sequencing data. The student shall be provided opportunities to:
>   (A) classify objects by comparing similarities and differences;

REQUIREMENT FOR PROMOTION

In order to be eligible for promotion, students will be required to master 70% of the essential elements for each subject area listed.

ENGLISH LANGUAGE ARTS
ESSENTIAL ELEMENTS

LISTENING

___ 1 Listens and responds to oral communications
  - nonverbal cues
  - sounds of letters of the alphabet and rhyming words
  ___ • main idea of a passage read orally
  ___ • response to storytelling by drawing or painting

SPEAKING

___ 1 Uses oral language fluently and effectively
  - creative dramatics and nonverbal communication
  - word variety in expressing feelings and ideas

READING

___ 1 Uses word attack skills
  ___ • basic phonics
  ___ • structural analysis
  ___ • sight vocabulary
  ___ • context clues
___ 2 Develops vocabulary to understand written material
  ___ • appropriate vocabulary used in complete sentences
  ___ • words in context
  ___ • alphabetical order according to initial consonant
___ 3 Uses comprehension skills
  ___ • main idea
  ___ • facts and details
  ___ • sequence of events
  ___ • fantasy and fact
  ___ • cause and effect relationships

    • clear and appropriate speech
    • ideas shared in group discussions
___ 2 Speaks to accomplish a variety of purposes
    • oral sequencing of events
    • choral reading of poetry
    • oral persuasion

WRITING
___ 1 Selects topics and generates material to write about those topics
___ 2 Writes effectively for a variety of purposes, modes, and audiences
    • stories and brief descriptions
    • first drafts to express ideas
___ 3 Applies the conventions of writing
    • spelling
    • capitalization and punctuation
    • handwriting-manuscript letters

    • predicting outcomes
___ 4 Applies reading skills to a variety of situations
    • following directions
    • oral reading
    • parts of a book
___ 5 Develops literary appreciation skills
    • repetition, rhyme, and rhythm
    • various forms of literature
    • variety of selections, characters, and themes
    • books for personal reading
    • story line involving several characters
    • time and setting of a story
    • feelings and emotions of characters

LANGUAGE
___ 1 Develops skills in using correct grammar effectively in both oral and written communications
    • singular and plural forms of regular nouns
    • regular verbs

FIGURE 6.1
Example of a report card using a checklist format

CHECKLIST

LEVEL I

Name _____ Date _____

Math
Age _____ Teacher _____ Unit _____

Advisor _____

<u>Dates</u>

I	M

NUMERATION

_____ _____ 0. Knows vocabulary:

_____ same _____ different _____ more _____ less _____ before _____ after
_____ _____ 1. Rote Counts:

_____ 1 ____ 2 ____ 3 ____ 4 ____ 5 ____ 6 ____ 7 ____ 8 ____ 9 ____ 10
_____ _____ 2. Count Objects:

_____ 1 ____ 2 ____ 3 ____ 4 ____ 5 ____ 6 ____ 7 ____ 8 ____ 9 ____ 10
_____ _____ 3. Match equivalent sets with concrete objects.
_____ _____ 4. Reproduce equivalent sets with concrete objects.
_____ _____ 5. Match like pairs
_____ _____ 6. Match unlike pairs
_____ _____ 7. Compare non-equivalent sets with concrete objects
_____ _____ 8. Reproduce non-equivalent sets with concrete objects
_____ _____ 9. Sorts objects using more than one classifying characteristic
_____ _____ 10. Match numerals:
_____ 1 ____ 2 ____ 3 ____ 4 ____ 5 ____ 6 ____ 7 ____ 8 ____ 9 ____ 10
_____ _____ 11. Identify numerals:
_____ 1 ____ 2 ____ 3 ____ 4 ____ 5 ____ 6 ____ 7 ____ 8 ____ 9 ____ 10
_____ _____ 12. Constructs sets for numerals:
_____ 1 ____ 2 ____ 3 ____ 4 ____ 5
_____ _____ 13. Names numerals:
_____ 1 ____ 2 ____ 3 ____ 4 ____ 5

MEASUREMENT

A. Linear
_____ _____ 1. Match objects
_____ size _____ length _____ width _____ height
_____ _____ 2. Compare objects
_____ size _____ length _____ width _____ height
_____ _____ 3. Seriates objects
_____ size _____ length _____ height _____

B. Weight
_____ _____ 1. Classify objects according to weight
_____ heavy _____ light
_____ _____ 2. Compare objects according to weight
_____ heavy _____ light
_____ _____ 3. Demonstrate use of balance
_____ _____ 4. Identify instruments for measuring weight

FIGURE 6.2
Mathematics checklist: level 1

114

> (B) classify objects from the environment as being living or nonliving; and
> (C) arrange events in sequential order
> (4) Experience in oral and written communication of data in appropriate form.
> The student shall be provided opportunities to:
> (A) describe objects from the environment; and
> (B) describe external features of organisms (pp. 22–23)

Preschool developmental checklists and curriculum checklists in the elementary grades are used in the same manner for the same purposes; however, developmental checklists add the developmental dimension to curriculum objectives (Wortham, 1984). Because the young child's developmental level is an important factor in determining the kinds of experiences the teacher will use, our discussion of the purposes of checklists will include the implications of child development during the early childhood years. Those purposes are as follows:

1. To understand development
2. To serve as a framework for curriculum development
3. To assess and evaluate development and learning

Checklists As a Guide to Understand Development

All developmental checklists are organized to describe different areas of growth, including social, motor, and cognitive development. The checklist items in each area for each age or developmental level indicate how the child is progressing through maturation and experiences. When teachers, caregivers, and parents look at the checklists, they can not only trace the sequence of development, they can also be realistic in their expectations for children. See, for example, the Frost-Wortham Developmental Checklist (Wortham, 1984) in Figure 6.4.

Checklists As a Guide to Develop Curriculum

Because developmental checklists describe all facets of development, they can also serve as a guide in planning learning experiences for young children. Curriculum is not necessarily described as content areas such as science, art, or social studies, as these are commonly organized in elementary school; rather, it follows the experiences and opportunities that young children should have in the early childhood years. Thus, teachers and caregivers who study the objectives on the checklists have guides for learning activities that will be appropriate for their children.

Because checklists are organized by developmental level or age, they also serve as a guide for sequencing learning. Teachers can match the experiences they wish to use with the checklist to determine whether they are using the correct level of complexity or difficulty. They can determine what came before in learning or development and what should come next. The skills sequence for Conceptual Development for *Happily Ever After,* the readiness level of the Addison-Wesley Reading Program (Rowland, 1982) (Figure 6.3), includes concepts for location terminology, descriptive terminology, temporal terminology, and relationships. By studying the range of concepts to be taught, the teacher can plan to teach those concepts within her instructional program using both the materials supplied with the Addison-Wesley program and the experiences she has designed for the children.

Developmental checklists help teachers and caregivers plan for a balance of activities. With the current emphasis on academic subjects even in preschool programs, teachers feel compelled to develop an instructional program that is limited to readiness for reading, writing, and mathematics. Preschool teachers are caught between the emphasis on "basics" and developmentally appropriate instruction that recognizes that young children learn through active learning based on interaction with concrete materials. Developmental checklists help the preschool teacher maintain a perspective between developmentally appropriate instruction and pressures to prepare children for first grade. Inclusion of developmental experiences helps the teacher ensure a balanced curriculum that is best for the children's level of development.

In planning the curriculum and instruction in early childhood or preschool programs, teachers must incorporate the use of learning centers in classroom experiences. Developmental checklists with a sequence of objectives provide guidelines for selecting the materials to place in centers to support curriculum and instruction. For example, for 5-year-olds, the sequence on a checklist for fine motor development might be similar to the following:

Cuts and pastes creative designs
Creates recognizable objects with clay
Ties shoes
Puts together a 20-piece puzzle
Creates or copies a pegboard design
Copies letters
Can copy numerals (Wortham, 1984, p. 33)

By studying the sequence, the teacher can determine that activities for cutting and pasting should be part of center activities earlier in the year. Later, when fine motor skills are better developed, opportunities to copy letters and numerals should be included in centers to complement instructional activities in writing. Thus, developmental checklists help teachers decide what to select for learning centers as the year progresses. Early in the year, the teacher may introduce simple toys, puzzles, and construction materials in centers. Later, more complex, challenging activities and materials are more appropriate. As the year progresses, the materials available in the centers should be compatible with their developmental growth.

Because the rate of development varies from child to child, the sequence of development reflected in the checklists allows the teacher to vary materials for individual children. Certain games, activities, or materials can be placed in the centers and designated for a particular child's needs or interests. Materials for experiences placed in centers provide a means of individualizing learning, with

FIGURE 6.3
Addison-Wesley Reading Program Skills Sequence

Left panel

Skill	1	2	3	4	5	6	7	8	9	10
Auditory Discrimination (cont'd)										
discriminate between same and different beginning sounds in words								X	•	
identify rhyming words										X
Auditory Memory										
to recall a sound	X									
to recall a series of directions			X	•						
Aural Comprehension										
follow oral directions	X	•	•	•	•	•	•	•	•	•
listen to a story for a purpose	X	•	•	•	•	•	•	•	•	•
recall details from a story	X	•	•	•	•	•	•	•	•	•
infer details from a story	X	•	•	•	•	•	•	•	•	•
identify character traits and mood in a story	X	•	•	•	•	•	•	•	•	•
identify sequence in a story	X	•	•	•	•	•	•	•	•	•
identify cause and effect in a story	X	•	•	•	•	•	•	•	•	•
identify main idea in a story								X	•	•
predict outcomes									•	X
CONCEPTUAL DEVELOPMENT										
identify location terminology:										
across	X	•	•	•	•	•	•	•	•	•
under	X	•	•	•	•	•	•	•	•	•
over		•	X	•	•	•	•	•	•	•
around		X	•	•	•	•	•	•	•	•
in, on		X	•	•	•	•	•	•	•	•

Right panel

Skill	1	2	3	4	5	6	7	8	9	10
Conceptual Development (cont'd)										
identify descriptive terminology:										
top, bottom, middle				X	•	•				
in front of, in back of, next to, between, behind				X	•	•				
first, next, last					X	•	•			
left, right						X	•			
up, down								X		
above, below								X		
identify descriptive terminology:										
same, different	X	•								
big, large, medium, little, small			X	•						
round							•			
happy, sad, angry, surprised						•				
long, short					•					
wide, thin							X			
more							X	•	•	•
identify temporal terminology:										
first, next, last						X	•			
identify relationships:										
categories				X	•	•	•			
parts of a whole									•	•
rhyming										X
FINE MOTOR SKILLS										
use marking devices	X	•	•	•	•	•	•	•	•	•
to underline	X	•	•	•	•	•	•	•	•	•
to draw a line across	X	•	•	•	•	•	•	•	•	•
to draw a line over			X	•	•	•	•	•	•	•
to circle										X

Note: An X indicates initial introduction. Dots indicate reinforcement.

Source: P. Rowland, *Happily Ever After*, 1982, Menlo Park, California: Addison Wesley Publishing Co.

checklists serving as the guide for a sequence from simple to complex. The more complex concepts or objectives lead to the selection of materials for the child whose development is more advanced.

Checklists As a Guide to Evaluate Learning and Development

Having information on how children are growing and learning is one of the important requirements of an early childhood program. Teachers must know how children's development and learning are progressing and must be able to discuss it with parents, other teachers, and staff members of other schools that may later teach the child. Figure 6.4 is an example of a checklist that may be used to evaluate a child's social development (Wortham, 1984).

Because the checklists cover all kinds of development, they also allow teachers to keep track of individual children and groups of children. When teachers keep consistent records on individual children, they can give parents information about the child's progress. Parents then have a clear idea of what is happening in school and what their child is accomplishing.

Teachers who use developmental checklists to assess, evaluate, and record children's progress may eventually realize that they have a better understanding of each child in the class than they had before. If a teacher uses a checklist for gross motor skills to keep track of large muscle development in his students, systematic observation of students engaged in physical activities will make the teacher more aware of how each child is progressing and reveal individual differences in development. When reporting to one child's parent, for example, the teacher may discuss the improvement in throwing and catching a ball. In another case, he may focus on the child's ability to ride a bicycle or to jump rope.

EVALUATING AND ASSESSING WITH CHECKLISTS

If a checklist is used as a framework for curriculum development and instruction, it can also be used for evaluation and assessment. The curriculum objectives used to plan instructional experiences can also be used to evaluate the children's performance on the same objectives. After a series of activities is used to provide opportunities to work with new concepts or skills, the children are assessed to determine how successful they were in learning the new skill or information. Evaluation can be accomplished through observation, during ongoing learning activities, and through specific assessment tasks.

Evaluating Checklist Objectives by Observation

Observing young children is the most valuable method of understanding them. Because children in early childhood programs are active learners, their progress is best assessed by watching their behaviors rather than using a test. If you look at the items on developmental checklists, you will see that some objectives or

FROST WORTHAM DEVELOPMENTAL CHECKLIST

SOCIAL PLAY AND SOCIALIZING
PRESCHOOL*

Color code: Green

LEVEL III	Introduced	Progress	Mastery
1. Engages in independent play			
2. Engages in parallel play			
3. Plays briefly with peers			
4. Recognizes the needs of others			
5. Shows sympathy for others			
6. Attends to an activity for ten to fifteen minutes			
7. Sings simple songs			
LEVEL IV			
1. Leaves the mother readily			
2. Converses with other children			
3. Converses with adults			
4. Plays with peers			
5. Cooperates in classroom routines			
6. Takes turns and shares			
7. Replaces materials after use			
8. Takes care of personal belongings			
9. Respects the property of others			
10. Attends to an activity for fifteen to twenty minutes			
11. Engages in group activities			
12. Sings with a group			
13. Is sensitive to praise and criticism			
LEVEL V			
1. Completes most self-initiated projects			
2. Works and plays with limited supervision			
3. Engages in cooperative play			
4. Listens while peers speak			
5. Follows multiple and delayed directions			
6. Carries out special responsibilities (for example, feeding animals)			
7. Listens and follows the suggestions of adults			
8. Enjoys talking with adults			
9. Can sustain an attention span for a variety of duties			
10. Evaluates his or her work and suggests improvements			

*Developed by Joe Frost and Sue Wortham. Used by permission of Joe L. Frost.

FIGURE 6.4
Frost Wortham Developmental Checklist
Source: Wortham, 1984.

120

CHAPTER 6

indicators of development can be evaluated only by observing the child. For example, in the area of language development, if a teacher wants to know whether a child is using complete sentences, he observes the child in a play activity and listens for examples of language. Likewise, if the teacher is interested in evaluating social development, she will observe the children playing outdoors to determine whether they engage mostly in solitary or parallel play, or whether individual children play cooperatively as part of a group.

Observation can be incidental or planned. The teacher may decide to do evaluations during center time and decide which items on a checklist can be evaluated by observing children in the art center or manipulative center. The teacher then places materials in those centers that are needed to observe specific behaviors and records which children are able to use the materials in the desired manner. For example, the ability to cut with scissors can be assessed by having a cutting activity in the art center. As an alternative, the teacher might use a cutting activity with an entire group and observe how each child is performing during the activity.

Evaluating Checklist Objectives with Learning Activities

Some objectives cannot be assessed through observation alone. Objectives in a cognitive area such as mathematics may require a specific learning activity for evaluation. However, instead of having a separate assessment task, the teacher can have children demonstrate their performance on a particular skill as a part of the lesson being conducted. He notes which children demonstrate understanding of the concept or mastery of the skill during the lesson. If a mathematics objective to be assessed involves understanding numbers through 5, the teacher might instruct a small group of children to make groups of objects ranging from one to five and note which children are successful.

Evaluating Checklist Objectives with Specific Tasks

Sometimes, at the beginning or end of a year or grading period, the teacher will want to conduct a systematic assessment. He will assess a series of objectives at one time. In this situation, the teacher determines a number of objectives that can be evaluated at one time and devises tasks or activities to conduct with a child or a small group of children. The activities are presented in the same fashion as in a lesson, but the teacher has the additional purpose of updating and recording progress. Assessment tasks are organized based on children's previous progress and will vary among groups of children. Some children will perform one group of activities; others will have a completely different set of activities related to a different set of objectives.

There is a time and place for each type of evaluation. The more experience a teacher has in including assessment in the instructional program, the easier it becomes. It is important to use the easiest and least time-consuming strategy whenever possible.

STEPS IN CHECKLIST DESIGN

A checklist is an outline or framework of development and curriculum. When designing a checklist, the developer first determines the major categories that will be included. Thereafter, development follows four basic steps:

1. identification of skills to be included
2. separate listing of target behaviors
3. sequential organization of the checklist
4. record keeping

Identification of the Skills to Be Included

The teacher studies each checklist category and determines the specific objectives or skills that will be included. Using established developmental norms or learning objectives, the teacher decides how to adapt them for his needs. For example, on a checklist for language development and reading under the category of Language and Vocabulary, the following objectives might be included:

Listens to and follows verbal directions
Identifies the concept of word
Identifies the concept of letter
Invents a story for a picture book

Separate Listing of Target Behaviors

If a series of behaviors or items are included in an objective, the target behaviors should be listed separately so that they can be recorded separately (Irwin & Bushnell, 1980). For the objective of identifying coins, the best way to write the item would be as follows:

Identifies:
>   penny
>   nickel
>   dime
>   quarter

When the teacher is assessing the child's knowledge of coins, he may find that the child knows some of the coins, but not others. Information can be recorded on the mastery status of each coin.

Sequential Organization of the Checklist

The checklist should be organized in a sequential manner. Checklist items should be arranged in order of difficulty or complexity. If the checklist is correctly sequenced, the order of difficulty should be obvious. For example, the ability to count on a mathematics checklist might be listed as "Counts by rote from 1 to

CONFLICTS ABOUT INFORMAL ASSESSMENT RESULTS

Mary Howell and Francesca Carrillo are having a heated argument in the teacher's lounge. Mary is a first-grade teacher, and Francesca teaches second grade. At issue is the checklist from the first grade that is placed in students' folders at the end of the year before they are promoted to second grade. Francesca's complaint is that the first-grade teachers' assessments are inaccurate. They have indicated that students accomplished first-grade objectives, but these objectives have to be retaught in the second grade because the students either never know them or forget them over the summer.

Mary is clearly offended that her professionalism has been questioned. She defends the process by which first-grade teachers determine whether the children have learned the objectives. Josie, another teacher sitting nearby, says nothing. Under her breath, she mutters, "It's all a waste of time. I wait until the end of the year and then mark them all off, anyway."

After Mary and Francesca have left, the conversation about the merits of using checklists for assessment and record keeping continues. Margaret Ramsey, a third-grade teacher, supports the use of checklists for evaluating the students. She observes that she uses the checklist record when having conferences with parents. She feels that the parents gain a better understanding of what their child is learning in school when she can tell them how the child is progressing on curriculum objectives listed on the checklist. Lily Wong, another third-grade teacher, strongly disagrees. Her experience with the checklists leads her to believe that record keeping takes a great deal of time that she would rather be using to plan lessons and design more interesting and challenging learning activities for her students.

10." At the next higher level, the checklist item would be "Counts by rote from 1 to 50."

Record Keeping

A system of record keeping must be devised. Because a checklist indicates the objectives for curriculum development or developmental characteristics, it must have a method of recording the status the items. Although many record-keeping strategies have been used, there are commonly two columns to indicate that the child either has or has not mastered the skill or behavior. Two types of indicators that are frequently used are a simple *Yes/No* or *Mastery/Nonmastery.* Another approach is to record the date when the concept was introduced and the date when it was mastered. In this instance, the columns would be headed by *Introduced/Mastery* or could indicate an intermediate step in evaluation with three columns headed by *Introduced/Progress/Mastery.* Figure 6.5 illustrates a checklist with two columns for record keeping in motor development. In this example, the columns indicate when the assessment was conducted. The codes $N = Needs$ *Improvement* and $S = Satisfactory$ are used to indicate the child's progress in mastery (Capon, 1975).

The teacher can use a checklist to record individual or group progress. Whether the teacher uses observation, lesson activities, or tasks for assessment, the checklist is used to keep a record of the child's progress. Checklist information

MARKING N = Needs Improvement S = Satisfactory	Task 1 Identify body parts		Task 2 Walking board		Task 3 Hopping		Task 4 Jump and land		Task 5 Obstacle course		Task 6 Ball catch		Task 7 Optional	
NAME	Fall	Spr.	Fall	Spr.	Fall	Spr.	Fall	Spr.	Fall	Spr.	Fall	Spr.	Fall	Spr.
1														
2														
3														
4														
5														
6														
7														
8														
9														
10														
11														
12														
13														
14														
15														
16														
17														
18														
19														
20														
21														
22														
23														
24														
25														
26														
27														
28														
29														
30														

Photo copy this page to make your own record sheet.

FIGURE 6.5
Perceptual Motor Evaluation Scale: record sheet
Source: Capon, 1975.

can be shared periodically with parents to keep them informed about what their child is learning or is able to do.

Checklists can also be used to keep a record of all of the children in the class or group. The group record lists all of the children's names, as well as the checklist objectives. By transferring information about individual children to a master or group record, the teacher can plan instruction for groups of children as the group record indicates their common needs. Figure 6.6 illustrates a checklist record for a group of students in language development.

ADVANTAGES AND DISADVANTAGES OF USING CHECKLISTS

There are definite advantages to using checklists for assessment and evaluation; there are also disadvantages or problems. Teachers have to weigh both sides when deciding how extensively they will use checklists for measurement and record-keeping purposes.

Advantages of Using Checklists

Checklists are easy to use. Because they require little instruction or training, teachers can quickly learn to use them. Unlike standardized tests, they are available whenever evaluation is needed.

Checklists are flexible and can be used with a variety of assessment strategies. The teacher can evaluate in the most convenient manner and obtain the needed information. Because of this flexibility, the teacher can combine assessment strategies when more than one assessment is indicated.

Behaviors can be recorded frequently; checklists are always at hand. Whenever the teacher has new information, he can update records. Unlike paper-and-pencil tests or formal tests, he does not have to wait for a testing opportunity to determine whether the child has mastered an objective.

Disadvantages of Using Checklists

Checklists can be time-consuming to use. Particularly when teachers are just beginning to use checklists, they report that keeping records current on checklists reduces the time spent with children. Teachers have to become proficient in using checklists without impinging on teaching time.

Teachers may find it difficult to get started. When they are used to teaching without using checklists, teachers often find it difficult to adapt their teaching and evaluation behaviors to include checklists. In addition, teachers can have too many checklists. They become frustrated by multiple checklists that overwhelm them with assessment and record keeping.

Some teachers may not consider assessment strategies used with checklists as valid measures of development and learning. For some teachers, particularly those in the primary grades, who are used to conducting a test for evaluation, the observation and activity strategies used to measure progress may seem inconclusive. They may feel the need for more concrete evidence of mastery of learning objectives for accountability.

Checklists do not indicate how well a child performed. Unlike a paper-and-pencil test that can be used to record levels of mastery, checklists indicate only whether the child can perform adequately. For teachers who are required to give grades at the elementary level, checklists can be an incomplete strategy for assessment (Irwin & Bushnell, 1980).

Checklists themselves are not an assessment instrument. They are a format for organizing learning objectives or developmental indicators. The teacher's implementation of evaluation strategies using a checklist makes it a tool for eval-

NAME	LANGUAGE ABILITY													FOLLOWING DIRECTIONS			
	1. Shares personal experiences	2. Voluntarily participates	3. Voluntarily answers	4. Tells observed activity	5. Answers factual questions	6. Answers probing questions	7. Answers higher order questions	8. Answers divergent questions	9. Problem solving	10. Asks factual questions	11. Interprets story picture	12. Comprehension	13. Attention span	14. Follows simple directions	15. Carry messages	16. 2 or more directions	17. Make simple object with specified materials

FIGURE 6.6
Language arts: class record sheet

uation. In addition, recording the presence or absence of a behavior is not the main purpose of the checklist. The significant factor is what the teacher does with the assessment information recorded. If the information gained from evaluating the objectives is not used for instructional planning and implementation followed by further ongoing evaluation, the checklist does not improve learning and development.

RATING SCALES

Rating scales are similar to checklists; however, there are important differences. Whereas checklists are used to indicate whether a behavior is present or absent, rating scales require the rater to make a qualitative judgment about the extent to which a behavior is present. A rating scale consists of a set of characteristics or qualities to be judged, using a systematic procedure. There are many forms of rating scales; numerical and graphic rating scales seem to be used most frequently.

Types of Rating Scales

Numerical Rating Scales
Numerical rating scales are among the easiest to use. The rater marks a number to indicate the degree to which a characteristic is present. A sequence of numbers is assigned to descriptive categories. The rater's judgment is required to rate the characteristic. One common numerical system is as follows:

> 1-unsatisfactory
> 2-below average
> 3-average
> 4-above average
> 5-outstanding

The numerical rating system might be used to evaluate classroom behaviors in elementary students as follows:

1. To what extent does the student complete assigned work?
   1   2   3   4   5
2. To what extent does the student cooperate with group activities?
   1   2   3   4   5

Numerical scales become difficult to use when there is little agreement on what the numbers represent. The interpretation of the scale may vary.

Graphic Rating Scales
Graphic rating scales function as continuums. A set of categories is described at certain points along the line, but the rater can mark his judgment at any location on the line. Commonly used descriptors for graphic rating scales are:

never
seldom
occasionally
frequently
always

The classroom behaviors described earlier would be evaluated on a graphic rating scale as follows:

1. To what extent does the student complete assigned work?
   never   seldom   occasionally   frequently   always
2. To what extent does the student cooperate with group activities?
   never   seldom   occasionally   frequently   always

The behavioral descriptions on graphic rating scales are more easily used than numerical descriptors. Because the descriptors are more specific, raters can be more objective and accurate when judging student behaviors; nevertheless, graphic rating scales are also subject to bias because of disagreement about the meaning of the descriptors.

Uses of Rating Scales

One of the most familiar uses of rating scales is on report cards. Schools often use them to report characteristics of personal and social development on a report card. Such attributes as work habits, classroom conduct, neatness, and citizenship commonly appear on elementary school report cards. Students and parents often feel that such ratings are particularly subject to teacher bias and feelings about the student.

An example of a rating scale is given in Figure 6.7. Taken from the *Early Childhood Environment Rating Scale* (Harms & Clifford, 1980), the page pictured shows a numerical scale for rating how the early childhood teacher provides for sand/water play and dramatic play, as well as the quality of the daily schedule.

ADVANTAGES AND DISADVANTAGES OF RATING SCALES

Rating scales are a unique form of evaluation. They serve a function not provided by other measurement strategies. Although some of the limitations of rating scales have already been discussed, it is useful to review their strengths and weaknesses.

Advantages of Using Rating Scales

Rating scales can be used for behaviors not easily measured by other means. In the area of social development, for example, a scale might have indicators of cooperative behavior. When the teacher is trying to determine the child's ability to work with children and adults in the classroom, the scale of indicators is more usable than a yes/no response category on a checklist. Unlike an observation,

Item	Inadequate 1 2	Minimal 3 4	Good 5 6	Excellent 7	SAMPLE SCORING STRIP
24. Sand/water	No provision for sand or water play.	Some provision for sand or water play outdoors *or* indoors.	Provision for sand and water play outdoors *or* indoors including toys (Ex. cups, spoons, funnels, shovels, pots and pans, trucks, etc.). Used at least weekly.	Provisions for sand and water play outdoors *and* indoors with appropriate toys.	24. Sand/water 1 2 3 4 5 6 7
25. Dramatic play	No special provisions made for dress-up or dramatic play.	Dramatic play props focused on housekeeping roles. Little or no provisions for dramatic play involving transportation, work, or adventure.	Variety of dramatic play props including transportation, work, adventure, fantasy. Space provided in the room and outside the room permitting more active play (either outdoors or in a multipurpose room or gym).	Everything in 5 plus pictures, stories, trips, used to enrich dramatic play.	25. Dramatic play 1 2 3 4 5 6 7
26. Schedule	Routine care (eating, sleeping, toileting, etc.) takes up most of the day. Little planning for interesting activities either indoors or outdoors.	Schedule is *either* too rigid leaving no time for individual interests *or* too flexible (chaotic) with activities disrupting routines.	Schedule provides balance of structure and flexibility. Several activity periods, some indoors and some outdoors, are planned each day in addition to routine care.	Balance of structure and flexibility, with smooth transitions between activities (Ex. materials ready for next activity before current activity ends). Plans included to meet individual needs (Ex. alternative activity for children whose needs differ from group).	26. Schedule (creative) 1 2 3 4 5 6 7

FIGURE 6.7

Examples from the Early Childhood Environment Rating Scale

Source: Reprinted by permission of the publisher from Harms, Thelma, & Clifford, Richard M., EARLY CHILDHOOD ENVIRONMENT RATING SCALE. (New York: Teachers College Press, © 1980 by Thelma Harms & Richard M. Clifford. All rights reserved), p. 29.

which might be completely open-ended, the rating scale indicators have clues to behaviors that describe the child's level of cooperation.

Rating scales are quick and easy to complete. Because the rater is provided with the descriptors of the child's behavior, it is possible to complete the scale with a minimum of effort. The descriptors also make it possible to complete the scale some time after an observation. The user can apply knowledge about the child after an observation or as a result of working with the child on a daily basis and will not always need a separate time period to acquire the needed information.

A minimum of training is required to use rating scales. The successful rating scale is easy to understand and use (Southeastern Day Care Project, 1973). Often paraprofessionals in schools can complete some rating scales. The scale's indicators offer the information needed to complete the scale.

Rating scales are easy to develop and use. Because descriptors remain consistent on some rating scales, teachers find them easy to design. When using rating indicators such as "always," "sometimes," "rarely," or "never," the teacher can add the statements for rating without having to think of rating categories for each one. Figure 6.8 shows a sample of cognitive behaviors for 3-year-olds measured on the rating scale, *Evaluating Children's Progress: A Rating Scale for Children in Day Care* (Southeastern Day Care Project, 1973).

Disadvantages of Using Rating Scales

Rating scales are highly subjective; therefore, rater error and bias are common problems. Teachers and other raters may rate a child based on their previous interactions or on an emotional rather than an objective basis. The subsequent rating will reflect the teacher's attitude toward the child (Guilford, 1954).

Ambiguous terms cause rating scales to be unreliable sources of information. Raters disagree on the descriptors of characteristics. Therefore, raters are likely to mark characteristics using different interpretations. For example, it is easy to have different interpretations of the indicator "sometimes" or "rarely."

Rating scales tell little about the causes of behavior. Like the checklists that indicate whether the behavior is present or absent, rating scales provide no additional information to clarify the circumstances in which the behavior occurred. Unlike observations that result in more comprehensive information about the context surrounding behaviors, rating scales provide a different type of information than checklists, but include no causal clues for the observer unless notes are taken beyond the rating scale itself.

SUMMARY

Informal evaluation measures are useful for teachers who need specific information about their students to use when planning instruction. Checklists and rating scales are informal instruments that can be designed and used by teachers to obtain specific diagnostic and assessment data that will assist them in developing learning experiences for their children.

THREE-YEAR-OLDS RATING FORM (From Age Three to Age Four)
(Rate at six-month intervals)

Cognitive

1. Compares size — Extends "matching" concept to size, as "big" or "little." Comparisons may be easy, but should be verbalized. *Child chooses between two items-- "Show me the little block" (spoon, doll, etc.), "the big block."*

2. Counts three — Extends concept of counting to three. Understands process of counting beyond two. May rote count beyond this. *Ask child to "hand me three pieces of candy from the bowl" (or three blocks from the pile).*

3. Dramatizes — Acts out, singly or with others, simple stories, Mother Goose rhymes and characters and scenes. Acts out role playing. *May make up from book or story that group has been reading.*

4. Uses plurals — *Take into account that the 's' may sound different if the child comes from a different cultural or language background.*

5. Converses — In short sentences, answers questions, gives information, repeats, uses language to convey simple ideas.

6. Sings — Sings short snatches of songs *Songs such as "Happy Birthday" or "Jingle Bells" pass. At least one chorus or verse.*

FIGURE 6.8
Sample of the Southeastern Day Care Project Rating Scale
Source: Southeastern Day Care Project, 1973.

130

Checklists are used for more than assessment or evaluation. They are a form of curriculum outline or a framework of curriculum objectives. With checklists, teachers can plan instruction, develop learning center activities, and evaluate children's progress and achievement on specific objectives.

Rating scales allow teachers to evaluate behaviors qualitatively. Raters can indicate the extent to which the child exhibits certain behaviors.

Checklists and rating scales are practical and easy to use. Teachers can develop them to fit the curriculum and administer them at their convenience. Unlike standardized tests, checklists and rating scales are current and provide the teacher with immediate feedback on student progress.

There are also disadvantages to using checklists and rating scales. Because they are not standardized, they are subject to error and teacher bias. Checklists do not include the level or quality of performance on the objectives measured. Rating scales, in particular, are subject to rater bias. Rating scale descriptors are ambiguous in definition. Differing interpretations of descriptors by raters lead to different responses and interpretations of children's behaviors.

Summary Statements

1. Checklists developed for early childhood programs usually include characteristics of development, as well as curriculum objectives.
2. Developmental checklists are organized to include social, motor, and cognitive development.
3. Developmental checklists serve as guides to the sequences of development and curriculum.
4. Developmental checklists serve as a guide for developing a balanced curriculum.
5. Checklists can be evaluated through observation, routine lesson activities, and specific assessment tasks.
6. Effective design results in more efficient use of checklists for evaluation and record keeping.
7. Checklists must have a record-keeping system that indicates the child's progress and/or mastery of checklist behaviors.
8. Rating scales require the rater to make a qualitative judgment about the extent to which a behavior is present.
9. Two rating scales that are most commonly used are numerical and graphic rating scales.
10. Rating scales are easy to use; however, they are also subjective and subject to rater error and bias.

REVIEW QUESTIONS

1. Describe the different functions of checklists. How can they be used by teachers for purposes other than evaluation or assessment?

2. Why is it important to use developmental checklists in early childhood programs?

3. How do developmental checklists serve as a guide for the sequence of development and curriculum?

4. Explain the different strategies that teachers can use to measure progress with checklist objectives.

5. How does the design of a checklist affect its use as an evaluation instrument?

6. What is sequenced organization in checklist design?

7. What methods can be used to record assessment results on checklists? Which form is best?

8. Why do some teachers have difficulty in using checklists? Do you see any solution to their problems?

9. How do rating scales differ from checklists?

10. Why are rating scales vulnerable to rater error and bias?

11. Is it better to use numerical rating scales or graphic rating scales? Why?

KEY TERMS

developmental checklist   numerical rating scale

graphic rating scale

REFERENCES

Capon, J. J. (1975). *Perceptual motor development. Basic movement activities*. Belmont, CA: Pitman Learning.

Gronlund, N. E. (1985). *Measurement and evaluation in teaching* (5th ed.). New York: Macmillan.

Guilford, J. P. (1954). *Psychometric methods* (2nd ed.). New York: McGraw-Hill.

Harms, T., & Clifford, R. M. (1980). *Early environment rating scale*. New York: Teachers College Press.

Irwin, D. M., & Bushnell, M. M. (1980). *Observational strategies for child study*. New York: Holt, Rinehart & Winston.

Morrison, G. S. (1988). *Education and development of infants, toddlers, and preschoolers*. Glenview, IL: Scott, Foresman.

Rowland, P. (1982). *Happily ever after*. Menlo Park, CA: Addison-Wesley.

Southeastern Day Care Project. (1973). *Evaluating children's progress: A scale for children in day care*. Mt. Rainier, MD: Gryphon House.

Texas Education Agency. (1985). *State Board of Education rules for curriculum: Principles, standards, and procedures for accreditation of school districts*. Austin, TX: Author.

Wortham, S. C. (1984). *Organizing instruction in early childhood*. Boston: Allyn and Bacon.

7

Informal Measures: Classroom and Teacher-Designed Tests and Assessments

The final type of evaluation to be discussed is teacher-designed assessments. In assessing and evaluating children from birth through the primary grades, measures other than paper-and-pencil tests are generally more appropriate. However, as children progress through the primary grades, they develop skills in reading and writing that will make it possible for them to demonstrate learning on a written test. In this chapter, we will discuss how teachers design their own assessments of classroom instruction and use commercially designed classroom tests.

PURPOSES OF TEACHER-DESIGNED ASSESSMENTS AND TESTS

Although all types of evaluation, both formal and informal, are used to measure and evaluate children's behavior and learning, there are circumstances in which teacher-designed assessments or written classroom tests are especially useful for the teacher. Paper-and-pencil tests, when given to students who are able to use them, can supplement other forms of evaluation and provide teachers with information that the other forms lack. These purposes include providing objective data on student learning and accountability and providing additional information in making instructional decisions.

Teacher-designed assessments supplement other evaluation measures, enabling the teacher to make more accurate decisions for the instruction of individual students. The teacher uses observation, tasks during group instruction, and manipulative activities to determine the child's progress in learning. A written test used with older children can reinforce or support the teacher's evaluation with an objective assessment. Objective testing complements the teacher's more subjective, personal evaluation, which can be subject to individual impressions or biases.

Classroom assessments can also support teachers' decisions that may be questioned by parents or school staff members. The teacher may understand, from ongoing work with a child, that the child needs to be instructed at a different level or requires extended experiences with a concept that other children have mastered. Although the teacher is confident in making the decision, a paper-and-pencil assessment can support it and, at the same time, help the parent to understand the nature of the problem. The teacher-designed assessment can thus increase the teacher's accountability for decisions that affect students' learning.

Teachers must make instructional decisions, both immediate and long-term. As they teach, they must decide how long to spend on a particular science unit or math concept. In addition to using informal evaluation strategies such as individual tasks and ongoing observations of class progress, they can use written tests to provide more information that will help them decide whether to include more experiences, use review activities, skip planned activities, or conclude the current topic and move on to a new one.

Unfortunately, at present, there is an increased emphasis on grading young children. Although kindergarten children may be exempt, primary grade students are being given letter or numerical grades in many schools, and the practice is expanding with the recent emphasis on higher instructional and grading standards. Teachers find it difficult to assign letter grades to primary school children. Whether the practice should continue is debatable; nevertheless, testing can help the teacher make decisions about student achievement. To use only written evaluations for grading would be inappropriate for all the reasons discussed throughout this book; however, when combined with other developmentally appropriate evaluation strategies, paper-and-pencil tests add supporting information on which grades can be based.

In the same fashion, tests can be used to support diagnostic decisions about student needs. The classroom teacher can supplement information from standardized tests and informal evaluations to determine student strengths and weaknesses in content areas. Assessments can be designed that correspond to local instructional objectives and provide specific information on student accomplishment and instructional needs. Once diagnostic information has been analyzed, the teacher can place students more accurately in instructional groups and regroup periodically as students move through the program at different rates.

Finally, teacher-made assessments allow evaluation of the local instructional program. Unlike standardized tests, which reflect general objectives suitable for a broad range of school programs at a state, regional, or national level, the teacher-designed test assesses specific or local learning objectives. These objective-based tests evaluate more closely the effectiveness of the local educational program. Without evaluation measures designed for the classroom, there is no ready method to assess local curriculum objectives.

TYPES OF TESTS USED WITH PRESCHOOL AND PRIMARY-GRADE CHILDREN

Teacher-designed assessments for preschool children must match the way that they learn—through active interaction with concrete materials. Children who do not yet read cannot demonstrate their learning effectively with a paper-and-pencil test. The teacher constructs assessment activities that allow the child to manipulate materials, explain understanding orally, or point to the correct response if expressive language is limited.

Teacher assessments using tasks or oral responses can be conducted during a teaching activity, as part of a learning center experience, or as a separate assessment or series of assessments (Wortham, 1984). For example, for the objective of recognizing uppercase and lowercase letters, the teacher may present a set of cards with five letters and ask the child to match the uppercase and lowercase letters. Figure 7.1 pictures an array of cards that can be used for this purpose.

To demonstrate an understanding of counting, the preschool child is given objects to count. The teacher can conduct the assessment in two ways. She may either select five objects and ask the child to count them, or she may ask the child to group five of the objects.

Pictures can also be used for assessment tasks with nonreaders. To assess knowledge of shapes, a pictured array of basic shapes could be used. If the objective is to identify shapes, the teacher can ask the child to find a given shape by saying, "Show me a triangle." The teacher can also point to the shape and ask the child to name it if the objective is to be able to name shapes. Figure 7.2 shows an array of shapes that can be used to identify circles, squares, triangles, and rectangles (Wortham, 1984).

For some preschool assessments, an oral response may be most appropriate. For example, a common preschool objective is for the child to know his first and last name. The teacher would ask the child to give this information.

For the objective of sequencing events in a story, the teacher shows the child a set of three to five pictures that have a logical sequence and asks the child to put them in order. The child is then asked to tell the story. Figure 7.3 shows a series of pictures that can be used for sequencing the cards and providing a verbal description.

As children learn to read, the teacher's assessments begin to include printed test activities with pictures and some written words. Instead of a physical re-

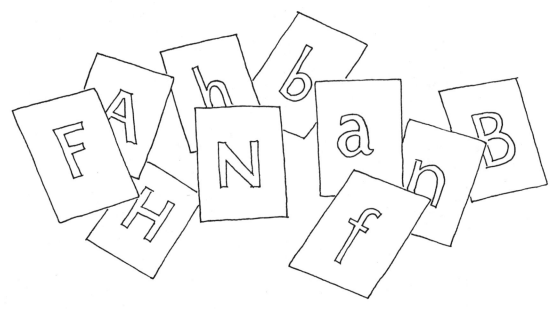

FIGURE 7.1
Uppercase and lowercase letters

sponse using concrete materials or an oral response, the child uses a pencil with a printed test. These written assessments can be commercially produced materials designed for classroom use with basal textbooks or as supplementary resources. The teacher must also be able to design her own tests to evaluate her own or individual learning objectives most effectively.

Paper-and-pencil tests must be adapted to the child's limited reading and writing skills. Therefore, tests designed for children in the primary grades use a format that provides pictorial or visual clues to assist the student in selecting or writing the correct response. To prepare beginning readers and writers for written tests, the teacher introduces key words such as *circle* or *draw* that are commonly used in paper-and-pencil assessments. More words are taught until the child is able to read written instructions. Throughout the primary grades, the teacher will introduce the assessment page with the children before asking them to complete the page independently.

When the student successfully completes a written assessment, the teacher may use a commercially prepared activity or design her own. Regardless of which type is chosen, there are certain tasks that are used to accommodate the child's limited reading and writing abilities. The most common tasks include marking or circling a response, drawing a line to a response, or writing simple numeral or word answers. Although both commercial and teacher-designed tests use these responses, the following examples are from commercial sources. Later in the chapter, the process of preparing teacher-designed assessments and tests will be described.

Children can circle pictures in response to questions before they have learned to read and write. This type of response is continued in the grades where beginning reading skills are acquired. Figure 7.4 (Payne et al., 1985, p. 107) demonstrates a commercially designed test in which the child is asked to circle the correct responses. In this figure the child is asked to circle the shapes that correspond with a given shape in a mathematics evaluation. The example is from a second-grade text.

A similar type of response can be made by marking a test question with an X or bubbling in an answer. Figure 7.5 (Rockcastle, McKnight, Solomon, & Schmidt, 1984, p. 79) uses a multiple-choice format. The child must mark the correct box with an X.

Matching by drawing a line from one figure to another can be used in the early grades in various content areas. Figure 7.6 (Rockcastle, McKnight, Solomon, & Schmidt, 1984, p. 75) shows the use of this test in a science unit on weather.

The child can be expected to write a correct response. In the examples given, the words are provided as clues to be used when selecting and writing the correct word. In Figure 7.7 (Rockcastle, McKnight, Solomon, & Schmidt, 1984, p. 72), a science test, the child looks below the blank in a sentence and selects the correct word to write in the blank. To respond, the child must be able to read the sentence and determine which word fits the context of the statement.

Although each of the examples given has been taken from a commercially designed test, teacher-designed tests follow the same or similar formats. Not only must the child have visual clues to be able to respond, an example is usually given to help the child understand the task. Also, although there are written instructions for the child to read, in reality the teacher may need to read and discuss the

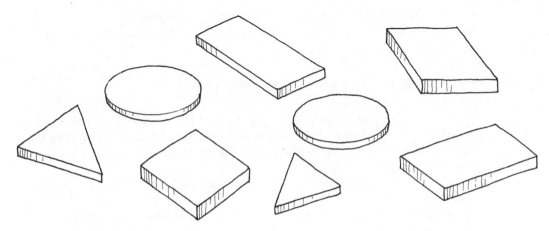

FIGURE 7.2
Array of basic shapes

FIGURE 7.3
Sequencing pictures

instructions with the students to ensure that they understand what is required. In the following section, we discuss the design of teacher-constructed assessments and tests.

HOW TESTS ARE DESIGNED AND USED

Classroom tests are closely matched to curriculum objectives and content. Whether they are designed by the teacher or obtained from a textbook or other commercial source, they are used to measure the student's ability to benefit from classroom instruction.

      Unlike standardized tests that provide general information about student achievement, classroom tests measure student accomplishment and learning needs in relation to specific classroom objectives. Classroom tests can be used for placement and diagnosis, formative testing, and summative testing (Gronlund, 1985).

Name _____

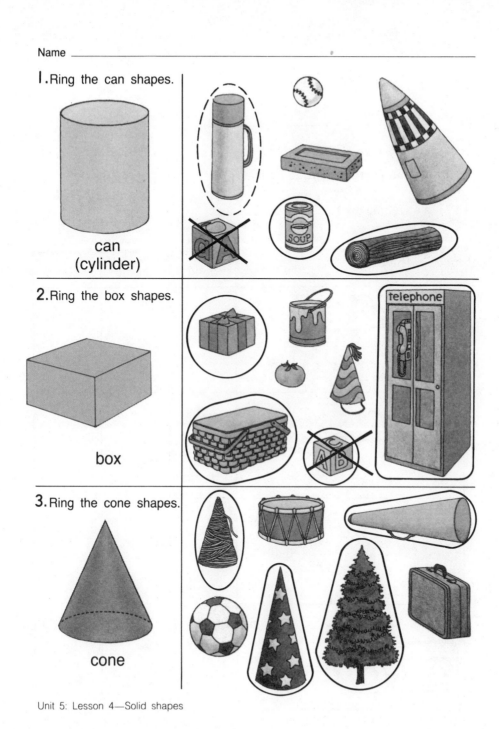

1. Ring the can shapes.

can
(cylinder)

2. Ring the box shapes.

box

telephone

3. Ring the cone shapes.

cone

Unit 5: Lesson 4—Solid shapes

FIGURE 7.4

Circling the correct answer

Source: From *Harper & Row Mathematics, Teacher's Edition, Grade* 2 by J. N. Payne et al. New York, Macmillan, 1985. Used by permission of Macmillan Publishing Co.

Matter

Name _____

Choose the best word to finish the sentence.

1. All things on earth that take up space

   and have weight are _____.

   solids   matter

Is it a solid, liquid, or gas?
Put an X in the box.

		Solid	Liquid	Gas
2.	milk			
3.	carrot			
4.	air inside balloon			
5.	wagon			

FIGURE 7.5
Putting an X on the correct answer

Source: Addison-Wesley Science Teacher's Resource Book by V. N. Rockcastle, B. McKnight, F. Solomon and
V. Schmidt 1984, p. 79. Copyright 1984 by Addison-Wesley Publishing Company, Inc. Used by permission.

CHAPTER 4

Weather

Name _____

Draw a line from each activity to the kind of weather
that would be best for doing it.

1.

   sledding

hot

2.

   selling umbrellas

snowy

3.

   swimming

windy

4.

   spray painting

calm

5.

     sailing

rainy

FIGURE 7.6
Drawing a line to the correct answer

Source: Addison-Wesley Science Teacher's Resource Book by V. N. Rockcastle, B. McKnight, F. Solomon and
V. Schmidt 1984, p. 75. Copyright 1984 by Addison-Wesley Publishing Company, Inc. Used by permission.

CHAPTER 2

Chapter Test **72**
Page 2

Living Things in Fall and Winter

Name ______________________________

Write the answer on each blank.

1. Winter is the ________________ time of year.
   coldest warmest

2. Some plants die in winter.

   New plants of this kind grow from ________________.
   seeds leaves

3. Some plants do not lose all their leaves in winter.

   They are called ____________________.
   winter greens evergreens

4. Some animals ____________________ before winter.
   hatch babies lay eggs

5. Some animals store food for ________________.
   summer winter

6. Beavers store ______________ under water.
   nuts sticks

7. In winter, some animals ____________________.
   move away make fires

8. Some animals rest all ________________.
   winter summer

72 Level 2 • Chapter 2 • Use at the end of Chapter 2.

FIGURE 7.7
Writing a word for a response

Source: *Addison-Wesley Science Teacher's Resource Book* by V. N. Rockcastle, B. McKnight, F. Solomon and V. Schmidt 1984, p. 72. Copyright 1984 by Addison-Wesley Publishing Company, Inc. Used by permission.

Placement and diagnostic testing have a similar function. In placement testing, the student is assessed to determine the instructional group in which he should be placed. Tests are given to determine what the student already knows and is ready to learn. Diagnostic testing is used to determine student weaknesses that need to be corrected. The same tests can be used for both purposes unless learning difficulties are persistent and need more extensive diagnosis by the school diagnostician or psychologist. Placement and diagnostic testing in the classroom are similar to criterion-referenced testing using standardized tests; however, the tests may assess selected learning objectives rather than objectives for an entire grade level.

Formative and summative testing are related to Mastery Learning (Bloom, Madaus, & Hastings, 1981). Formative tests are given periodically while teaching specific objectives to monitor student progress. These tests measure a limited number of objectives at a time so that the teacher can identify which objectives have been mastered and which call for additional work or activities. They provide feedback and are not used for grading purposes.

The **summative test,** in contrast, is the final test that is given on completion of a unit of work. The unit of work may be organized for a single objective or for a small group of objectives. The summative test is given after instruction and formative testing reveal that the material has been mastered. It is administered as the final step to verify the student's achievement on the material covered in the unit or group of objectives.

The information gained from diagnostic, placement, formative, and summative testing provides the teacher with current, relevant information for instructional planning. It allows the teacher not only to group students for instruction effectively, but also to determine how long the class needs to continue working on objectives and whether alternative types of experiences are needed to correct learning weaknesses in particular students. Unlike standardized tests that are administered once a year, classroom tests provide ongoing, criterion-related information about student progress on objectives being covered in a particular classroom. To use classroom testing effectively, the teacher must know how to design appropriate tasks that match the students' ability to use paper-and-pencil tests. The teacher must also know what kinds of tests will accurately measure the students' progress or mastery of each learning objective.

STEPS IN TEST DESIGN

Teacher-designed classroom evaluations, although less rigorously constructed than standardized tests, must accurately measure objectives for classroom instruction. Whether the teacher is organizing assessment strategies for preschool or primary-school students, tests are carefully designed to fit the learning objectives. Although this section of the chapter discusses teacher assessment in terms of test design, it refers to evaluation strategies for preschool students who are nonreaders, as well as for students in the primary grades who are beginning to read and write.

There are several steps in test design that must be followed if the test is to measure student learning accurately. Based on Bloom's model of Mastery Learning (Bloom, 1974), the process includes the following:

1. Determination of instructional objectives
2. Construction of a table of specifications
3. Design of formative and summative evaluations
4. Design of learning experiences
5. Design of correctives and enrichment activities

Determining Instructional Objectives

In Chapter 5, we discussed objectives relative to skills continuums and checklists. The same types of sources are used to develop instructional objectives that will be used to design classroom tests. School districts have various sources to draw from when determining curriculum objectives for each grade level.

One common source of curriculum objectives is basal textbook series used in the classroom. Most textbooks in reading, mathematics, social studies, and science are based on learning objectives that are appropriate for that grade level in school districts in many states. There is a commonly accepted pool of learning objectives in the content areas for each grade level; however, objectives can vary markedly among different basal series. Textbooks are organized around these objectives, and teachers' editions of the textbooks contain activities to implement instruction for the objectives and tests to evaluate student learning on the objectives.

School districts, particularly large, urban ones, establish their own learning objectives in various content areas for each grade level. These objectives may draw on commercial resources, which are supplemented with other objectives that are deemed important in the school district.

The state education agency may produce learning objectives for each grade level in each content area. The state-mandated curriculum objectives are followed by each school district. These objectives may be the minimum required by the state. If this is so, local districts may have the freedom to supplement state learning objectives with commercial and local sources for additional objectives.

The *Addison-Wesley Mathematics Teacher's Edition* for first grade (Eicholz, et al., 1985) includes sets of skills that are divided into 14 chapters or units. Chapter 2 of the text covers "Sums to 5." The objectives for the unit are as follows:

2.1 Recall addition facts through sums to 5.
2.2 Solve problems using cumulative computational skills.

The teacher using this textbook can use these objectives, plus others, to determine the learning objectives for mathematics in the first-grade classroom. The objectives will be followed in designing instructional experiences and testing procedures to evaluate achievement.

Writing Behavioral Objectives

Before a learning objective or outcome can be measured, it must be stated clearly in terms of its content and the desired behavior. The content refers to the knowledge or skill to be learned. The behavior is what the student does to demonstrate that the knowledge or skill has been attained (Gronlund, 1985). In the objectives described previously, the content is clearly stated, but the required behavior is missing. Objective 2.1, "Recall addition facts through sums to 5," describes the required skill but does not specify how the student will demonstrate it. If the statement is changed to read "The student will recall addition facts through sums to 5 by correctly adding sums in 10 problems," the desired behavior has been described.

Analyzing Objectives to Determine Prerequisite Skills

The teacher must not only develop the learning objective, but must determine what must be taught for the student to master it. Part of the planning for instruction involves studying the learning objective to decide what prior knowledge or skill the student must have to be able to learn the new information. In objective 2.1, "Recall addition facts through sums to 5," the teacher will plan instruction to help students learn to combine all possible groups of numbers that equal 5. In addition, the teacher determines what the student must already know to understand and use addition skills. Prior skills to be considered include the following:

1. Knowledge of numbers through 5
2. Identification of numerals through 5
3. Understanding that small groups can be combined to make a larger group

The teacher must decide whether the students have the prerequisite skills to be able to master the targeted learning objective. If not, the prior skills will have to be taught, or retaught if necessary, before the new objective is introduced. A pretest or diagnostic test may be used to determine student readiness for the learning objective.

Setting a Standard for Mastery

The final step in determining the instructional objectives is to set the level of mastery that will be expected for the student to learn the objective. The level of accomplishment may be set by the teacher, the school district, or the state education agency. This is the minimum standard required to pass the objective. The learning objective can reflect the established standard for mastery. If 80 percent is established as the minimum standard for mastery, the learning objective can be stated to reflect the standard. Objective 2.1, the mathematics objective for first grade, can be rewritten to include the standard of mastery as follows: "The student will be able to recall addition facts through sums to 5 by correctly completing 8 of 10 addition problems." If each objective does not include the written standard of mastery, the standard can be set separately for all of the learning objectives.

Constructing a Table of Specifications

When learning objectives for a unit of study or the content of an entire course have been described behaviorally, the teacher or curriculum developer is ready to outline the course content. Before a test can be organized to measure the curriculum objectives, it is necessary to understand more accurately what concepts or skills are to be measured and to what extent the student will be expected to perform to demonstrate mastery of the objective. Will the student be expected to remember information, use the information to solve problems, or evaluate the information? The test items will reflect the level of understanding that is required to master the objective.

Analysis of objectives to determine the level of understanding is commonly done by constructing a **table of specifications** (Gronlund, 1985). Here learning objectives are charted using Bloom's *Taxonomy of Educational Objectives* (Bloom, 1956). This work describes levels of understanding in the cognitive domain ranging from the ability to recall information, or the knowledge level, to the highest level of understanding, evaluation. Figure 7.8 explains the levels of Bloom's Taxonomy with examples of terms that characterize each level. In Figure 7.9, an adaptation of the Taxonomy is used to make a table of specifications for the mathematics unit covering addition sums to 5. The two objectives for the unit are listed to the left of the figure. The columns to the right describe how the objectives are charted on the Taxonomy. The first objective requires that the student be able to recall addition facts and problems, understand the facts and problems, and be able to apply that understanding. The second objective also requires that the student be able to analyze or solve problems. When designing test or assessment items, the teacher must know the type and level of understanding that test items will reflect and must organize the test so that the described levels of understanding are adequately sampled. Figure 7.10 is a table of specifications for a unit on classification at the kindergarten level.

Designing Formative and Summative Evaluations

After the teacher has determined what is to be measured by designing a table of specifications for the learning objectives to be taught, it is time to design the formative and summative evaluations. Both types of evaluation are derived from the table of specifications. Assessment items will be designed to measure the student's achievement at the levels on Bloom's Taxonomy, as described on the table of specifications. The assessment items on the two forms are equivalent, but the evaluation purposes differ. The formative evaluation is not a test; it is a checkup or progress report on the student. The teacher uses the formative evaluation to decide whether the students need further work with the objective.

If the student needs additional experiences, more activities, known as **correctives,** are implemented. Correctives are learning resources designed to approach the objective differently from the original instruction. The intent is to provide various kinds of activities to meet individual students' needs.

Level of Understanding	Descriptive Terms	
Knowledge Recognition and recall The ability to remember or recognize information	Tell List Name	Define Identify Locate
Comprehension The ability to translate information in your own words Show that you understand	Restate Discuss Explain Review	Describe Summarize Interpret
Application The ability to use information or apply learning to new situations and real-life circumstances	Demonstrate Construct Imply	Dramatize Practice Illustrate
Analysis The ability to break down information into parts To identify parts of information and its relationship to the whole	Organize Differentiate Compare Distinguish	Solve Experiment Relate

Synthesize
The ability to assemble separate parts into a new
    whole
The ability to take information from various sources
    and present it in a created form
	Design
	Plan
	Develop
		Compile
		Create
		Compose

Evaluation The ability to make judgments about information To be able to evaluate based on criteria or standards	Decide Conclude Appraise	Judge Assess Select Choose

FIGURE 7.8
Explanation of Bloom's Taxonomy
Source: Bloom, 1956.

   If the student's responses indicate mastery on the formative evaluation, the teacher provides enrichment activities. The student engages in activities that are at a higher level on Bloom's Taxonomy than are required for mastery. Thus, if the mastery level on the table of specifications is at the application level, students who master the information after an initial period of instruction may benefit from activities at the analysis, synthesis, or evaluation levels (Bloom, Madaus, & Hastings, 1981).

   The summative evaluation is the final assessment or test of what the child has learned or accomplished. It is given after all instruction has been concluded. Although formative and summative evaluations are interchangeable in content,

Sums to 5	Know	Comprehend	Apply	Analyze	Synthesize	Evaluate
2.1 Recall addition facts through sums to 5	X	X	X			
2.2 Solve problems using cumulative computational skills	X	X	X	X		

FIGURE 7.9
Table of specifications for a unit on sums to 5

only the summative form is used as a test. The decisions to be made about both assessments include the format, selection of assessment items, determination of length, and assembly of the assessment.

Test Format

Earlier in the chapter, we talked about test formats for use with children in the primary grades. When the teacher is ready to design classroom tests, the appropriate format will have to be determined. Most preschool children respond best to concrete tasks and oral questions. With first graders, the teacher must limit student responses to tasks that require little or no reading and writing, such as circling pictures, marking the correct response, or drawing lines to correct responses. Later in the year, and for children in second and third grades, more writing and reading can be incorporated into the test format. If several different tasks are to be used, more than one format may be used for a test. Figure 7.11, designed for an assessment of a unit on money in the second grade, demonstrates the format used. The student must draw a line from the coin to its name and write the numerical value below the coin.

Assessment Items

In addition to determining the format or formats to be used in the assessment, the teacher must develop the items that reflect the table of specifications describing the objectives to be tested. Figures 7.12 and 7.13 are examples of an assessment that fulfills a cell of the table of specifications developed for the unit on coins. In Figure 7.12, Objective 5 requires the student to count collections of coins up to 99 cents. Figure 7.13 requires the student to count the value of the coins and record the total on the line provided with each of the eight collections of coins.

At the preschool level, Figure 7.10 shows a table of specifications for a unit on classification. Objective B specifies that the student will be able to remove the object that is different from a set of four objects. Figure 7.14 pictures a group of objects that may be used to evaluate the child's performance on the objective. The child chooses or points to the object that does not belong in the group.

Test Length

After determining the format and developing a pool of items to provide the levels of understanding expected from the table of specifications, the test developer must determine how many test items or tasks will be included in the test. For young children, a balance is reached between the number of items needed to demonstrate the child's responses to determine understanding and a reasonable length that will not overtax the young student's ability to attend to the task. For preschool and primary grades, the test length should not exceed the time normally needed to complete classroom activities and assignments. A maximum of 20 to 30 minutes is reasonable in testing primary-school students. Commercial tests designed to evaluate these students commonly are one page long.

Behavioral Objectives	Knowledge	Comprehension	Application	Analysis	Synthesis	Evaluation
A. Classifying 1. The student will describe the object by naming one of its attributes	X	X				
2. The student will construct a set from various objects by classifying together those with common attributes	X	X	X			
B. Noting Differences 1. From a set of four objects, the student will remove the one object that is different from the others	X	X	X	X		
C. Classifying by Name 1. The student will classify a group of pictures into two categories, using class names	X	X	X			
D. Classifying by Design 1. The student will classify objects into sets according to design, such as stripes, dots, etc.	X	X	X			

FIGURE 7.10
Unit objective: classifying objects by common attributes in a table of specifications

Assembly

The final step in test design is to assemble test items into both a formative and a summative form. The teacher should construct enough items so that both forms of the test can be put together at the same time. The formative evaluation, conducted after the students have had some work with the objective, will enable the teacher to assess how well the students are learning the information. After the formative assessment has been examined, the teacher can reteach, provide different types of experiences or practice for some students, or move on to the

Name._____ Summative Evaluation

Draw a line to match the coins with their names.

1.

quarter   nickel   half-dollar   penny   dime

2. Write the value of each coin on the line.

_____   _____   _____   _____   1 ¢

FIGURE 7.11
Teacher-designed test on coins

summative test if the students show adequate progress. The teacher should have enough items to get the feedback needed to monitor student learning and mastery. The formative and summative assessments should be equivalent in terms of the level of understanding required and the types of items used.

When assembling the tests, the teacher must decide how instructions will be given to the students. If written instructions requiring reading skills will be used, they must be simply stated to match the students' reading ability. Pictures used must be clear and easily interpreted. Poorly drawn or inappropriate pictures

OBJECTIVES	KNOWLEDGE	COMPREHENSION	APPLICATION	ANALYSIS	SYNTHESIS	EVALUATION
1. The student will be able to identify the five coins (half-dollar, quarter, dime, nickel, penny) by sight with 100% accuracy.	X					
2. The student will be able to match the five coins with their letter names with 100% accuracy.	X					
3. The student will be able to match the five coins to their number value using a cent sign (¢) with 100% accuracy.	X	X				
4. The student will be able to classify like coins by counting: pennies by ones, nickels by fives, dimes by tens, and quarters by twenty-fives, with 80% accuracy.	X	X	X	X		
5. The student will be able to differentiate like/unlike coins by switch counting from twenty-fives to tens to fives to ones in necessary order to count collections of coins up to 99¢ with 80% accuracy.	X	X	X	X		
6. The student will be able to analyze and solve story problems by counting coins with 80% accuracy.	X	X	X	X		

FIGURE 7.12
Unit on coins: table of specifications

Name _____

Count the coins. Write the
total on the line.

3.

31¢

4.

_____

5.

_____

6.

_____

7.

_____

8.

_____

FIGURE 7.13
Test on coins

will hamper the child's ability to respond correctly and distort the child's performance on the test. If the teacher is unable to draw simple pictures, she should obtain them from another source or ask a colleague for help.

Designing Learning Experiences

When the table of specifications and the formative and summative evaluations have been constructed, the teacher collects and prepares the activities and instruction that will enable the student to learn the information designed in the objective. Instruction also matches the level on the table of specifications. Instruction to introduce and work with the objectives includes teacher instruction and other resources normally used by the teacher to help children practice and master new concepts and skills.

Designing Correctives and Enrichment Activities

Corrective activities for students who need additional work after initial instruction and formative evaluation provide learning alternatives. These include audiovisual resources, games, workbooks, peer tutoring, student–teacher discussions, and other opportunities that are different from the original instruction and activities. The purpose is to provide different or alternative ways for the student to learn the information in the learning objective.

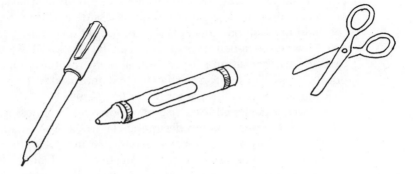

FIGURE 7.14
Unit on classification: array of objects

Enrichment activities are also different from the original instruction. They allow students who easily mastered the objective initially to engage in challenging and more creative activities. The students can work on individual projects that allow them to do problem solving and apply their own ideas in various types of activities that emerge from their own efforts (Block, 1977).

ADVANTAGES AND DISADVANTAGES OF USING TEACHER-DESIGNED EVALUATIONS

Teacher-designed assessments in the classroom have several advantages over commercially produced tests developed for the same purpose. The advantages are all related to the flexibility of the tests constructed for the teacher's own classroom.

When the teacher plans an assessment activity or test, the objective or objectives to be tested may be selected to suit individual class needs. Unlike commercial tests, which may be programmed to fit student progress in a grade-level textbook, the teacher-designed test can vary from the structure or plan of the book. A teacher may be concerned about an objective outside of the textbook sequence and feel compelled to conduct an evaluation. Because she is developing tests to fit classroom needs, the targeted objective can be tested within the teacher's assessment plans whenever needed.

In addition, teacher-constructed assessments can be designed for a particular class. If the children are nonreaders, but have advanced concepts that normally are introduced to children who have reading skills, the teacher can write the test to accommodate their abilities. If the students are advanced readers, the test can be designed to take advantage of their reading skills. The most common difficulty with commercial classroom tests is that they are set for a certain reading level or penalize the child for being unable to perform well because pencil-and-paper skills are required. The teacher can modify test tasks to include manipulative activities, oral responses, and assessment within instructional periods if the child understands concepts but cannot yet respond on a written test.

Teacher-designed assessments can be improved whenever needed. Each time the teacher administers a test, student responses provide feedback on its effectiveness. The test can be changed and improved whenever students' response indicates problems with the format or test items.

Teacher-designed tests also have potential weaknesses, which generally focus on the teacher's skill in designing classroom assessments. Because teachers do not generally have extensive experience in developing their own tests, the evaluations they design may not be effective in evaluating student learning.

Because of the abundance of commercially designed tests that accompany curriculum texts and kits, teachers are not always required to construct their own tests. Teachers become dependent on commercial tests and do not consider the necessity of designing their own. As a result, the teacher may not clearly understand the purpose of the tests or the levels of knowledge that are tested.

ASSESSMENTS FOR INSTRUCTIONAL OBJECTIVES: HOW USEFUL ARE THEY?

Norris teaches kindergarten. He and the other kindergarten teachers have been sent to a training session on designing assessments for instructional objectives using Mastery Learning. In the session, the teachers have reviewed how to write behavioral objectives and how to construct a table of specifications based on Bloom's Taxonomy of Educational Objectives. Working with the table of specifications prepared them to design assessment strategies for the objectives.

On the way home after the training session, Norris and the other teachers voice skepticism. How can this kind of testing be used with kindergarten children? Norris comments, "I can see how some areas, such as math, can be organized and assessed by behavioral objectives, but how do you decide what eighty percent accuracy is on learning the Pledge of Allegiance, or what they learn from art or using concepts in science?" Jane, another kindergarten teacher in the group, agrees in principle with the strategies they have learned. She remarks, "I can see why they want us to learn the process. It forces us to be more specific in our understanding of what the objectives are meant to accomplish. My problem is that I'm afraid that we are going to end up teaching to objectives and fragmenting the curriculum with the children."

Norris finally decides that it is a matter of common sense. The teacher can apply the strategies with some parts of the curriculum in kindergarten, but not others. The question is whether the school's principal and the kindergarten coordinator will share his perspective. He and the other kindergarten teachers decide to talk to teachers at other grade levels to determine how they are implementing the assessment strategies. Afterward they want to study their curriculum and decide where they can use assessments based on a table of specifications. They want to meet with the principal and coordinator to discuss where the process will work and which parts of the curriculum do not lend themselves to that type of assessment.

When Norris and the other teachers meet with the principal and the kindergarten coordinator, they present tables of specifications and assessments for mathematics and units in science. After they explain their reluctance to use the process with their reading program and other curriculum components, the kindergarten coordinator supports their position. The principal is more reluctant, but decides to let the coordinator work with the teachers to determine how and where the assessment strategies will be implemented at the kindergarten level.

Teachers may lack the training in test design that affects both the understanding of the purpose of the commercial tests and the skills needed to construct tests. For example, teachers may not have learned how to use a table of specifications for curriculum objectives. When they design tests, they are not aware of the levels of knowledge in the curriculum that need to be part of the evaluation process. This may be more true of early childhood teachers than of teachers in intermediate grades and secondary school. Teachers of preschool and primary-age children need to be aware of the various levels of cognitive understanding, as well as alternative methods of evaluation that are developmentally suited to young students.

Finally, the process of developing good classroom tests, especially for younger students, is time-consuming. Because test items must be developed to accommodate emerging reading and writing skills, each item must be carefully considered both for content and for method or format. This takes more time than developing items for students who have good reading and writing skills. The method of presentation is as important as the concepts and skills being tested.

A discussion of the weaknesses of teacher-designed assessments must include mention of the issues surrounding the use of Mastery Learning in early childhood education. Because Mastery Learning requires that the teacher analyze learning objectives and determine the level of mastery to be achieved, it would seem to be in conflict with the philosophy that early childhood educators should provide classroom experiences that are developmentally appropriate. That is, the teacher is encouraged to provide learning experiences that are consistent with the child's level of development, rather than ask the child to fit into a predetermined style of learning that requires specific types of responses to achieve mastery.

Certain components of the preschool classroom curriculum lend themselves to the Mastery Learning approach. Concept development, particularly in mathematics, has sequential objectives that can be taught within the Mastery Learning format. Nevertheless, many early childhood educators object to attempts to limit early childhood programs to this approach. The need for exploratory and inquiry-based experiences, originating from the child's opportunity to initiate activities both indoors and outdoors, using self-directed learning, is essential in early childhood classrooms. In fact, these experiences are essential for both preschool and primary-grade levels.

Teachers must ultimately be able to understand and use their own assessments appropriately to match the curriculum and their students' development. Mastery Learning must also be used appropriately in early childhood programs.

Despite their weaknesses, teacher-designed evaluations have an important place in early childhood classrooms. An answer to the difficulties in using these assessments may be to help teachers understand the process of test design and to support their efforts to develop tests.

SUMMARY

Although written tests are the least commonly used method of evaluating the learning of young students, there is a place for these tests once children have mastered some reading and writing skills. Teachers and parents can use written tests as sources of objective information of student progress.

Like standardized tests, teacher-designed and commercially produced classroom assessments are developed using procedures that ensure that they are correct in content and method of evaluation. Test design begins with careful analysis and description of learning objectives for the curriculum. The objectives are examined for the prerequisite skills that must be mastered prior to their use, and how the content and skills must be taught. In addition to determining the level of mastery for the learning objectives, the test developer must use a developmentally appropriate test format that will maximize the performance of students who are learning to read and write.

Before test items are constructed, the test designer must describe the level at which the student must demonstrate the new knowledge. A table of specifications organized for the learning objectives is used for this purpose. While constructing the formative and summative evaluations, the teacher must consider length, equivalent items for both evaluations, and what types of test instructions are most appropriate.

Because paper-and-pencil tests may not be the most effective way to evaluate or assess children through the primary grades, teachers must understand when and how such tests are appropriate. The teacher must have acquired the skills to develop such tests if they are to measure learning accurately and appropriately. Teachers of young students must also understand the limitations of written tests and become skilled in combining them with alternative evaluation methods to make sure that each student is tested with procedures that are most appropriate for his own level of development and ability to respond.

Summary Statements

1. Written classroom tests are another useful measure in testing children who are acquiring reading and writing skills.
2. Paper-and-pencil tests may be an objective source of student learning.
3. Assessments developed for children in the primary grades must use pictures and other visual cues to accommodate the limited reading and writing skills of these students.
4. Specific steps in test design are followed by teachers and other developers of classroom evaluations to ensure that they measure curriculum objectives accurately.
5. Design of written classroom assessments includes a table of specifications, formative and summative forms, and consideration of the length and format that are appropriate for testing preschool and younger elementary students.

REVIEW QUESTIONS

1. How do written tests serve a different purpose than other types of tests and evaluation methods?
2. Why should teachers be careful when using written tests with students in the primary grades?
3. How do written tests provide records of student learning that facilitate teaching accountability?
4. Why is the description of the content and student behavior important in using learning objectives for assessment design?

5. How does the standard of mastery affect both the learning objective and the test developed to measure achievement of the objective?

6. What is a table of specifications? How is it used with learning objectives?

7. Why do teachers need to understand the levels of knowledge used to chart objectives on a table of specifications?

8. Describe different formats that are used in written tests developed for beginning readers.

9. What kinds of guidelines should the teacher consider when determining the length of a test for primary-grade children?

10. Can more than one format be used in an assessment?

11. How are formative and summative tests alike? Different?

12. Why are written tests for primary-grade children difficult to design?

13. Why do classroom teachers tend not to develop their own tests?

14. How can teacher-designed tests be more effective than commercially designed tests that evaluate the same objectives?

15. When should teachers use written tests? When should they not use written tests?

KEY TERMS

correctives	summative test
formative test	table of specifications

REFERENCES

Block, J. H. (1977). Individualized instruction: A mastery learning perspective. *Educational Leadership, 34,* 337–341.

Bloom, B. S. (Ed.). (1956). *Taxonomy of educational objectives: The classification of educational goals. Handbook I. Cognitive Domain.* New York: McKay.

Bloom, B. S. (1974). An introduction to mastery learning theory. In J. H. Block (Ed.), *Schools, society and mastery learning.* New York: Holt, Rinehart & Winston.

Bloom, B. S., Madaus, G. F., & Hastings, J. T. (1981). *Evaluation to improve learning.* New York: McGraw-Hill.

Eicholz, P. E., O'Daffer, P., Fluxor, C., Charles, R., Young, S., & Barnett, C. (1985). *Addison-Wesley mathematics teacher's edition. Book I.* Menlo Park, CA: Addison-Wesley.

Gronlund, N. E. (1985). *Measurement and evaluation in teaching.* New York: Macmillan.

Payne, J. N., Beardsley, L., Bunch, B., Carter, B., Coburn, T., Edmonds, G., Payne, R., Rathmell, E., & Trafton, P. (1985). *Mathematics teacher's edition Grade 2.* New York: Harper & Row.

Rockcastle, V. N., McKnight, B., Solomon, F., & Schmidt, V. (1984). *Addison-Wesley science teacher's resource book. Level 2.* Menlo Park, CA: Addison-Wesley.

Wortham, S. C. (1984). *Organizing instruction in early childhood.* Boston: Allyn and Bacon.

8

Putting Measurement and Evaluation in Perspective: Looking Ahead

I n the preceding chapters, we studied the many methods used to measure young children. We have examined the strategies employed to learn about young children from birth through the early childhood years: how they grow and develop, how they learn, and how we can find out if there is a problem with development and learning.

In discussing each measurement and evaluation method, we considered the information that teachers, caregivers, and parents may want or need to know. This information included the purposes of the evaluation, how it is conducted, and why it is useful. Each topic was also discussed in terms of surrounding problems or issues, as well as the strengths and limitations of the test, particularly when used with young children.

In this chapter we go beyond these topics and consider how the programs that serve children can be measured. Many of the measurement strategies used to learn about children can be broadened or generalized to examine and evaluate programs. Program evaluation also includes measurement tools that do not directly involve testing children, but focus instead on evaluating how different components of the program have succeeded or need to be modified.

We also consider the status of issues and controversies related to testing and evaluating young children that may remain as significant concerns in the future. Many problems about the use of testing in the early childhood years have not

PROBLEMS IN MAKING PLACEMENT DECISIONS

Mr. Kreplick is attending a meeting for parents of kindergarten children. The principal is explaining the new policy on whether children will be sent to first grade from kindergarten or placed in a transitional first grade with a developmental curriculum for those who need more time before they enter first grade.

Timmy Kreplick has had problems adjusting to kindergarten all year, and his parents have been worried about what will happen to him next year in first grade. Mr. Kreplick is relieved to hear that the children will be tested in May. If the test shows that they are better suited for the transitional class, they will be placed there rather than in first grade. They won't experience failure.

Mrs. Standish, sitting next to Mr. Kreplick, questions the plan. What happens if a child matures over the summer? What happens if, in October, the child can do well in first grade? Will the child be moved to a regular first-grade class?

Because this is the first year of the transitional class, the principal has no answer. The school

will use a wait-and-see approach, monitoring the children to see how well they do during the year. One possibility that has been considered is to retest the children when school begins in September to reassess their abilities after the summer vacation. It is possible that a child will belong in first grade instead of the transitional class. It has also been suggested that the teacher in the transitional class will have a 6-week period with the children during which individual children can be reevaluated and placed in first grade if it appears that they can succeed.

Mr. Kreplick is less anxious about Timmy's progress next year. He is convinced that Timmy will need the program offered by the transitional class. Mrs. Standish is less sure about the program. She still has concerns about adding an extra year of school, whether it is a transitional class or retention in kindergarten. She is not convinced that the school district knows clearly what it hopes to achieve through the transitional first-grade classes. She also does not understand what is meant by a developmental curriculum.

been resolved. Where are we headed in addressing the issues of the misuse of testing with young children?

Finally, we will look at the teacher's role in the measurement and evaluation of young children. What are the teacher's responsibilities in using various measurement tools? Should the roles and responsibilities of teachers be altered or expanded? How will future measurement trends affect teachers and how they work with young children?

BEYOND MEASUREMENT AND EVALUATION OF YOUNG CHILDREN: THE ROLE OF PROGRAM EVALUATION

Throughout this book, we have referred to program effectiveness. Standardized tests were discussed not only for assessing student achievement, but also for determining strengths and weaknesses in the instructional program. In discussing testing of preschool children for developmental delays, we also mentioned that selection of intervention services and evaluation of their effectiveness are part of the overall plan for the child. Program evaluation involves the use of measurements to determine what works or doesn't work well in programs for young children. This information serves many purposes, which will now be discussed.

Purposes of Program Evaluation

The purpose or purposes of evaluating early childhood programs depend on the type of program and what one wishes to accomplish. Programs funded by a state, federal, or foundation source are required to submit yearly evaluation reports affirming that the projected results have been achieved. Accountability for program quality to meet regulation or accreditation standards also requires evaluation results. Child care centers regulated by state agencies must demonstrate that they maintain the minimum requirements for licensing. Evaluations must be done periodically to ensure that standards are observed. Public schools must evaluate their instructional programs to determine that standards for student learning have been met. They may also use program evaluation results to validate instructional quality for parents.

Program evaluation is performed to assist in the management, planning, and development of the program; for decision making and policy formation (Royce, Murray, Lazar, & Darlington, 1982); and for program assessment and improvement (Decker & Decker, 1988). Two types of evaluation, formative and summative, are used to determine whether the program is functioning effectively or has achieved its purpose.

Formative Evaluation

When a program is designed, the planning process includes developing objectives for each program component, such as the administration, curriculum, and budget. After the program is implemented, formative evaluations are done to assess progress and provide ongoing improvement (Royce, Murray, Lazar, & Darlington, 1982). Formative evaluation is used to determine whether the program is meeting its objectives and to correct any weaknesses discovered.

The effectiveness of curriculum experiences provided for young children can be monitored by studying such factors as equipment and materials, curriculum activities, and teacher behaviors. *The Early Childhood Environment Rating Scale* (Harms & Clifford, 1980) provides ongoing assessment of personal-care routines, equipment and furniture, language and reasoning experiences, fine and gross motor activities, creative activities, social development, and adult needs. Another measurement tool, *The Instrument Based Program Monitoring Information System* (Fiene, 1985) is designed to help early childhood centers meet state day care regulations, and the *Day Care Environmental Inventory* (Prescott, 1975) provides a system to gather information about physical space and descriptions of children's experiences. The staff can study the information to decide whether the activities observed met their expectations for the children and make adjustments in the program.

Administration and budget goals can also be monitored throughout a program. Program goals for administration may include the establishment of a computerized record-keeping system for payment of fees and expenses. Periodic monitoring during the year can be conducted to determine whether the goal is being met, and what needs to be done if the system is not being developed adequately and on time. The yearly budget can also be examined throughout the year to ensure that expenditures are not exceeding income and that funds are being spent for the purposes intended.

Each type of formative evaluation is designed to improve the program and to make corrections when objectives are not being achieved. Formative evaluation allows developers to investigate the program on a continuing basis. They are directed to be attentive to the progress of the program during the year, rather than discovering at the end that certain changes should have been made.

Summative Evaluation

Whereas formative evaluation is used to make adjustments so that program objectives can be met, summative evaluation measures the outcomes of a program (Decker & Decker, 1988). Summative evaluation is used to determine program effectiveness at the end of a set period by measuring overall program success and quality.

Federally funded programs are held accountable for reaching their objectives by the end of a funding year. Program developers must report program outcomes to the funding agency. Achievement tests may be administered to determine if students benefited from the program (Zigler & Valentine, 1979). In a nationally funded program such as Head Start, positive findings from summative evaluations may affect congressional decisions on future funding (Comptroller General of the United States, 1979).

Summative evaluation can also be used to assess research projects associated with early childhood programs. Evaluations are used to answer research questions about program effectiveness. Guralnick (1982) was interested in whether young handicapped children benefited more from mainstreamed programs than from segregated programs. Warger (1988) cited public school early childhood programs that have been validated as effective through research of program outcomes. Phillips (1987) reported on research conducted with child care centers that provided indicators of quality programs.

The Future of Program Evaluation

Program evaluation will continue to have a significant role. Awareness of the importance of programs for all populations of young children is growing at the local, state, and national levels. Program evaluation will expand as new programs are developed and the quality of existing ones is improved by the many individuals, groups, agencies, and institutions that will be involved in implementing early childhood programs.

As more parents seek child care, as well as educational programs, for their infants and preschool children, providers of these services become more competitive. Day care centers, churches, public schools, and private preschools are beginning to recognize that they must provide quality programs for both care and learning. Day care programs are moving from caregiving to more comprehensive services. Thus, centers providing daily care for young children now call themselves *child enrichment centers* or *early learning centers*, rather than *child care centers*.

Public schools also recognize that working parents need care for their children beyond regular school hours. Many schools now provide care before and after school to accommodate family needs. Parents will increasingly look for quality in the programs they select for their children. They will also be concerned about convenience. Many parents prefer to have their child remain at one location for the entire day. The overall quality of both care and learning will be a factor in deciding where to place their child. If early childhood programs wish to compete, they must constantly monitor the quality of their program compared to that of others in the area or community.

Whereas public schools will use local or state-designed program evaluation, other early childhood settings will seek validation of the quality of their programs through other means. The National Association for the Education of Young Children has developed a process whereby providers of early childhood programs and care can gain recognition for the quality of their program. Using the *Accreditation Criteria and Procedures of the National Academy of Early Childhood Programs* (1984), early childhood centers can attain accreditation through a national organization. As more programs seek accreditation, program evaluation will become a continuing process for centers and schools that previously did not conduct periodic assessments.

At the end of the 1980s, state and federal funding for early childhood programs began to expand after a cutback for several years. Expansion of future programs for children who are handicapped, gifted and talented, or at risk for learning deficits in the early childhood years will include provisions for accountability. Evaluation will be required to validate the quality of existing and new programs (Jennings, 1988).

As the need for programs and subsequent program evaluation increases, issues surrounding the testing of young children will continue to be a concern. The methods of measuring and testing young children will continue to be examined as educational reforms and new program development call for program evaluation strategies including the use of standardized testing and other measurement strategies.

RESOLVING THE ISSUES: FUTURE TRENDS

In the 1990s, no one is certain of all the trends that will develop in the measurement of young children and early childhood programs. Unresolved issues of the 1980s will remain as the education reform movement continues to affect children of all ages, both in school and in preschool years. These issues will include how to improve the quality of programs for young children, the developmentally appropriate curriculum for young children, the correct use of testing and measurement with young children, and the continuing need for research on program effectiveness.

Providing Quality Programs for Young Children

As the push to accelerate learning in response to calls for improved instruction clashes with efforts to ensure that young children are placed in classes with a developmentally appropriate curriculum, the struggle between the two forces is escalating. The problem of providing the best possible programs for young children within current restrictions is likely to continue for some time, with implications for how children will be tested and how frequently tests will be administered.

Part of the conflict focuses on developmental programs versus academic programs, sometimes referred to as the *push-down* curriculum. Warger (1988) described the problem as follows:

> Curriculums once intended for 1st grade have been moved to kindergarten and now are being moved into preschool. The assumption is that mastering a preschool academic curriculum will give young children an early jump on the academic curriculum they will face later on. (p. viii)

Day (1988) stated that we have accepted the proposition of fitting the child to the curriculum rather than designing the curriculum to meet the developmental needs of the child. Although research clearly indicates differently, the Early Childhood and Literacy Development Committee of the International Reading Association (1985) lamented that a heavy emphasis on children's academic development in kindergarten is replacing a more balanced curriculum. Katz (1988) commented on the emphasis of the first-grade curriculum in kindergarten classrooms: "This appears to me to be doing earlier and earlier what we don't do very well later" (p. 36). In spite of efforts to counter the increased academic emphasis in early childhood programs, this trend seems destined to continue in the foreseeable future.

The increased academic pressure on preschool and primary school students has resulted in a parallel increase in early school failure. Because preschool programs, particularly kindergartens, are not based on the development of young children, more children are failing. In an effort to prevent early school failure, educators are looking for alternatives, such as delaying entry into kindergarten, retention in kindergarten or first grade, and placement in a transitional class before or after kindergarten. Decisions about placement in the appropriate program result in screening and testing of children for developmental maturity, readiness, and school achievement. In *Kindergarten Policies: What Is Best for Children?* Peck, McCaig, and Sapp (1988) observed that "children are being tested before, during, and after kindergarten to determine whether they will be permitted to enter school, which class they will be placed in, and whether or not they will be 'promoted' " (p. 7).

The issues of retention and placement in transitional classes were discussed extensively in earlier chapters. Nevertheless, the fact remains that as long as we expect preschool children to learn primary school objectives using primary school strategies and materials, children will fail to fit the curriculum. Efforts to help children do better in school will involve increased testing. This change in concern from "continuity of development to a concern for continuity in achievement" (Spodek, 1981, p. 179) will have far-reaching effects on many young children in the future.

The increased use of testing, especially standardized testing, is another trend, at least for the near future. Many states have instituted state assessment systems to guide them in making educational reforms. Cohen (1988) stated that states should design assessments to meet their own needs. He also believed that state assessments might help to identify effective programs and indicators of quality in state schools.

Two major factors will fail to halt the downward spiral of elementary curriculum and the use of standardized testing. One is related to funding of preschool programs. Because many preschools are funded through sources that require accountability, standardized tests are necessary. The curriculum of the program becomes defined by the test so that good test results will ensure funding for the next year. Because the standardized tests available for use with children measure academic skills, the curriculum taught must prepare the child for success on the test (Karweit, 1988).

The other factor is the continuing effect of educational reform. Shepard and Smith (1988) stated that the downward shift of curriculum demands is likely to continue, because many see the academic emphasis in preschool classes as evidence of the success of educational reforms. As school districts and states broaden the use of standardized tests to evaluate the effect of educational reforms, the tests will continue to encroach on the kindergarten curriculum (Hiebert, 1988). Because existing tests such as the *Stanford Early Achievement Test* and *Metropolitan Readiness Test*, which are most frequently used, focus on academic skills, kindergarten programs will continue to stress instruction in those skills.

The use of standardized testing for making decisions about promotion and retention seems destined to continue as a side effect of school reform efforts. However, there are indications that some states are reconsidering this practice with younger children. Ezra Bowen reported in *Time* magazine (April 25, 1988) that 61 percent of children in the Norwood-Norfolk central school district in the state of New York failed a standard readiness test used for entry to kindergarten. The test was determined to have a 50 percent margin of error after the children had been assigned to a 2-year kindergarten program. Peck, McCaig, and Sapp (1988) remind us that research evidence indicates that readiness tests do not predict whether a child will succeed in kindergarten.

There is likely to be increased attention to the problem of placing children in transitional classes or retaining them in kindergarten because they are not considered ready for first grade. Shepard and Smith (1988) urged educators to find alternatives to labeling unready children as deficient. They proposed that continuing to screen children for school entry will deny public education to children who need it the most.

Karweit (1988) suggested that we must consider more viable alternatives to retaining children in kindergarten or assigning them to a junior first grade. She proposed that the preprimary school years be broken into smaller time units or that children be allowed to enter school during the quarter of the school year in which their birthday occurred. Both of these practices would introduce flexibility into the school year that might help to accommodate developmental variations. Nevertheless, regardless of what methods are used to assign children to classes, there will still be wide variations in development and preparation for academic learning. We hope increased efforts will be made to stop labeling children as deficient because they do not fit a prescribed level of development. Rather, school districts will focus on modifying preschool programs to best instruct their young students.

Some states are heeding the warning that formal instruction and standardized tests are not developmentally appropriate for kindergarten children. An article in *Education Week* (Gold, August 3, 1988) reported that the state of Mississippi was discontinuing the use of standardized tests with kindergarten children. The same article reported that North Carolina, Arizona, California, and Georgia were eliminating or modifying the use of standardized tests for kindergarten, and in two of the states for first- and second-grade children as well. Changes in testing practices may increase as educators respond to information about problems with standardized tests. Hiebert (1988) reported that changes in future tests will reflect an emergent literacy perspective. Teale (1988) and others will continue informing teachers how informal techniques can provide effective alternatives for assessing and evaluating young children.

There are also indications that advocates of developmentally appropriate early childhood programs will also be heard. Peck, McCaig, and Sapp (1988) cited 20 position statements concerning the need for developmentally appropriate kindergartens compiled from national and state organizations and agencies. These position statements were strong indicators that policy makers are being alerted to the problem and, hopefully, will respond in a manner that will benefit children in kindergartens and other early childhood programs.

Expanding Programs for Children with Special Needs in the Early Childhood Years

Public Law 94-142, the Education for All Handicapped Children Act of 1975, guarantees a free and appropriate public education for all handicapped children between the ages of 3 and 21, regardless of the type or severity of their handicap. This law made sweeping changes in public schools. It is perhaps the most important law affecting the young handicapped child. In previous chapters, we discussed how the law contributed to the development and use of measurement instruments for preschool children. Some of the tests designed and constructed in response to the law were described.

In the years to come, PL 99-457, passed in 1986, will have an equal impact on children in the early childhood years. The new law partially corrects some limitations of PL 94-142 and adds new services for young children.

Although PL 94-142 brought comprehensive services to children beginning at age 3, there were many who were not served. Obviously, children from birth to age 3 were not covered by the law. In addition, states were required to provide services between the ages of 3 and 5 only if they provided services to children of those ages who were not handicapped. If a state only provided kindergarten, or did not have a kindergarten program, public program services for preschool handicapped children might not be available.

Under PL 99–457, states applying for funds under PL 94–142 must demonstrate that they are providing a free public education to all handicapped children between the ages of 3 and 5. Beginning with the 1990–1991 school year, states no longer have the option of serving or not serving preschool handicapped children.

A federal Early Intervention Program, also part of PL 99-457, establishes services for handicapped infants and toddlers from birth to 2 years of age. The program provides early intervention services for infants and toddlers who are developmentally delayed. Because each state determines what constitutes developmental delay, there are significant implications for the development and use of additional tests for developmental screening and diagnosis of deficits. These services may also vary in quality from state to state.

Family services are also a part of PL 99-457. Program options serving handicapped infants and toddlers include part-day, home-based programs and part- or full-day center- or school-based programs. Individualized Family Services Plans (IFSP) must be designed by a team that includes the parents. A broad range of services must be provided to meet the child's developmental needs (Morrison, 1988). The IFSP includes a multidisciplinary assessment developed by the team and the parents. Caregivers, parents, and professionals will use observation and other informal assessments with standardized instruments to determine the child's developmental status. Checklists and rating scales will be used to help identify the characteristics that have developed normally. Once developmental delay is established, professionals on the team will conduct more intensive diagnostic tests before designing a plan for the child and family.

PL 99-457 is intended to expand services to preschool handicapped children. With the new interest in the early childhood years, it is hoped that services for preschool children through improved funding for Head Start, Day Care, and preschool programs for gifted and talented children will be expanded. When funding is available, such programs will probably have to document their effectiveness through evaluation.

THE ROLE OF TEACHERS IN THE SELECTION AND USE OF TESTS AND MEASURES USED WITH YOUNG CHILDREN

What is to be the role of classroom teachers in the selection and use of tests and other forms of measurement? Will teachers have more authority and responsibility for the measurement tools that will be selected for use in their classes?

In previous chapters, we described the design and construction of informal and formal measurement strategies, believing that teachers, caregivers, parents, and other school personnel involved with young children should be knowledgeable about the characteristics of various tests. In the case of standardized tests, we discussed how to evaluate and select tests to be used with young children.

Some of the tests discussed are used by teachers. Others, particularly psychological tests such as IQ tests, require extensive professional training and are administered only by psychologists, counselors, or diagnosticians. Teachers use observation, checklists and rating scales, and screening tests, as well as standardized tests such as achievement tests. They also design and use their own assessment tools. In evaluating handicapped children and those with learning disabilities and providing the necessary services, teachers work within a team of providers in conducting screening and testing.

The important point is that in the case of some standardized tests that teachers administer, they have no part in the decisions that are made when the tests are selected. When achievement tests are chosen for a school district, teachers are rarely included in the decision-making process. Readiness tests and other instruments used with preschool children are administered by teachers but rarely selected by them.

This situation leads to questions about the selection and use of tests. Should teachers who administer tests to young children be informed about their quality? Should they have a voice when the decision is made to test their students?

These questions may become issues in the future as the use of testing with preschool and primary-age children becomes more controversial and receives more publicity. As parents become more informed about questions that are being raised concerning the tests used to make decisions about grade placement, they will expect teachers to be able to explain the rationale for such tests. Will teachers themselves expect to be included when a decision is to be made about a testing procedure or instrument that affects the future of their students?

As school reform decisions increase the use of testing of preschool and primary grade children for placement, promotion, and retention, teachers will increasingly feel that they are accountable for their role in the decisions that are made about their students. If they disagree with the grading procedures they are required to use, for example, do they have a responsibility to voice their concern? When they have research-based information that an instrument is being used for the wrong purpose or lacks reliability, should they so inform the personnel in their district who selected the tests? Should teachers press for more informal methods of evaluation as alternatives to standardized testing? Hopefully, teachers will be encouraged by administrators to be informed and share that information so that appropriate testing methods and instruments will be used with the young students in their district or institution.

Teachers may also seek to be included in program evaluation. Research cited about retention and placement in transitional classrooms in earlier chapters demonstrated that there is little evidence that children placed in transitional classes do better than children who are promoted. Recent research (Jones, 1985; Shepard & Smith, 1987) supported the same conclusion. In addition, children retained in a grade do not generally do better than those who are promoted. Regardless of this research, however, school districts are continuing to establish more transitional classes. Should teachers be informed of the research on the effectiveness of transitional classrooms? Should school districts and states implementing additional transitional classrooms be conducting ongoing research on the effectiveness of these programs, which seem to be a trend for the future? Should teachers question their role in these programs and expect to be accountable to the parents that their instructional program has proven its effectiveness and quality through well-designed evaluation?

SUMMARY AND CONCLUSION

The measurement and evaluation of young children, which started at the beginning of this century, has broadened and intensified over the decades as more has been learned about how young children develop and learn, and how variances in development may cause young children to encounter difficulties when they enter school. Movements to provide services for preschool children such as Head Start, PL 94-142, and PL 99-457 have used the advances of the child study and testing movements to evaluate children for developmental delays and handicapping conditions. Tests and measures for the early childhood years have been developed in response to the need to identify young children who will benefit from intervention services and preschool programs that will enhance their academic success when they enter the primary grades.

Other measures have been developed to evaluate or assess the progress and achievement of children in preschool and primary programs. Procedures have been established to evaluate not only the children, but also the programs and schools that serve them.

The development and use of a variety of approaches to teaching and measurement of children in the early childhood years has many problems. Because of the nature and rapidity of development of young children, it is difficult to design measures that are dependable and that accurately measure personal characteristics and other needed information. Each kind of measure designed for use with these young children has pluses and minuses. Users of each type of measure must be informed about the strengths and limitations of the strategies they plan to use. With young children especially, a combination of measurement approaches is indicated, rather than a single instrument or method.

We have no crystal ball that reveals future trends in the measurement of young children. There are certain indicators, however. School reform, which is a national phenomenon, will continue to have an impact on early childhood education. At the same time that the importance of the early years is again being emphasized, the school reform movement is establishing restrictive parameters on the education of young children. The push for quality programs that are developmentally appropriate for young children is in conflict with efforts to raise academic standards. As a result, academic policies that are counter to the best educational programs for young children in the early childhood years are being forced on early childhood educators. The measurement and evaluation of young students and preschool children is and will continue to be both a cause and an effect of the forces that will characterize future early childhood programs.

The issues that surround the measurement and evaluation of young children will not be resolved soon. If present trends continue, there will be a parallel increase in the measurement of young children in the effort to improve their potential for optimum development and learning. Hopefully, the ongoing improvement in measurement methods and instruments will have a positive result for children in the early childhood services and programs yet to be designed.

Summary Statements

1. Standardized tests administered to young children are also used to measure program effectiveness.
2. Program evaluations are conducted to account for program quality, to account for adherence to state or national standards, and to assist in program management or administration.
3. Program improvement is a major purpose of program evaluation.
4. Formative evaluation of a program assesses progress in program goals, and summative evaluation measures program outcomes.
5. Standardized testing is likely to increase in the 1990s as the effect of educational reforms expands.
6. As larger numbers of children enroll in early childhood programs, new information about measurement and evaluation will be needed to provide better opportunities for learning.
7. Expansion of programs for children with special needs will extend services and provide them to the family as well as the child.
8. Teachers will need to play a significant role in selecting tests and other methods of measuring children in future early childhood programs.
9. Teachers and school district administrators will need to stay informed about research and current trends regarding the measurement and evaluation of young children to provide the best programs that meet the needs of these students.

REVIEW QUESTIONS

1. How do program evaluations affect the teacher's decisions about the classroom curriculum?

2. How can program evaluation results help improve instruction?

3. How can tests used for program evaluation control the teacher's method of instruction?

4. Why will program evaluation become more important in the future?

5. Why will the emphasis on academic skills in preschool classes continue to increase in the 1990s?

6. How can parents affect the types of early childhood programs that will be available in the 1990s?

7. Why are retention and transitional classes not the best alternatives for accommodating developmental differences in young children?

8. How will programs for children with special needs under PL 99-457 help more children than were served under PL 94-142?

9. How are parents more involved with the services provided to children under PL 99-457?

10. Will measurement and evaluation of young children increase or decrease in future years? Why?

REFERENCES

Bowen, E. (1988). Can kids flunk kindergarten? *Time,* April 25, 1988.

Cohen, M. (1988). Designing state assessment systems. *Phi Delta Kappan, 69,* 583–588.

Comptroller General of the United States. (1979). *Early childhood and family development programs improve the quality of life for low-income families. A report to the Congress.* Washington, D.C.: General Accounting Office, February 6.

Day, B. D. (1988). What's happening in early childhood programs across the United States? In C. Warger (Ed.), *A resource guide to early childhood programs.* Alexandria, VA: Association for Supervision and Curriculum Development.

Decker, C.A., & Decker, J. R. (1988). *Planning and administering early childhood programs* (4th ed.). Columbus, OH: Merrill.

Early Childhood and Literacy Development Committee of the International Reading Association. (1985). Literacy development and pre–first grade. A joint statement of concerns about present practices in pre–first grade reading instruction and recommendations for improvement. Newark, DE: International Reading Association.

Epstein, A. S. (1988). A no-frill approach to program evaluation. *High Scope Resource, A Magazine for Education,* Winter, 1, 12.

Fiene, R. (1985). The Instrument Based Program Monitoring Information System and the indicator checklist for child care. *Child Care Quarterly, 14,* 198–214.

Gold, D. L. (1988). Mississippi to end standardized tests for kindergarteners. *Education Week, 39,* 1, 32.

Guralnick, M. J. (1982). Mainstreaming young handicapped children: A public policy and ecological systems analysis. In B. Spodek (Ed.), *Handbook of research in early childhood education*. New York: Free Press.

Harms, T., & Clifford, R. (1980). *The Early Childhood Environment Scale*. New York: Teachers College Press.

Hiebert, H. E. (1988). The role of literacy experiences in early childhood programs. *The Elementary School Journal, 89,* 161–171.

Jennings, J. F. (1988). Working in mysterious ways: The federal government and education. *Phi Delta Kappan, 70,* 62–65.

Jones, R. R. (1985). *The effect of a transition program on low achieving kindergarten students when entering first grade*. Unpublished doctoral dissertation. Northern Arizona University, Flagstaff, Arizona.

Karweit, N. (1988). Quality and quantity of learning time in preprimary programs. *The Elementary School Journal, 89,* 119–134.

Katz, L. G. (1988). Engaging children's minds: The implications of research for early childhood education. In C. Warger (Ed.), *A resource guide to public school early childhood programs*. Alexandria, VA: Association for Supervision and Curriculum Development.

Morrison, G. S. (1988). *Education and development of infants, toddlers, and preschoolers*. Glenview, IL: Scott, Foresman.

National Association for the Education of Young Children. (1984). *Accreditation criteria and procedures of the National Academy of Early Childhood Programs*. Washington, D.C.: Author.

Peck, J. T., McCaig, G., and Sapp, M. E. (1988). *Kindergarten policies: What is best for children?* Washington, D.C.: National Association for the Education of Young Children.

Phillips, D. A. (Ed.). (1987). *Quality in child care: What does research tell us?* Washington, D.C.: National Association for the Education of Young Children.

Prescott, E. (1975). *Assessment of child-rearing environments: An ecological approach*. Pasadena, CA: Pacific Oaks College.

Royce, J. M., Murray, H. W., Lazar, I., & Darlington, R. B. (1982). Methods of evaluating program outcomes. In B. Spodek (Ed.), *Handbook of research in early childhood education*. New York: Free Press.

Shepard, L. A., & Smith, M. L. (1987). Synthesis of research on school readiness and kindergarten retention. *Educational Leadership, 24,* 346–357.

Shepard, L. A., & Smith, M. L. (1988). Escalating academic demand in kindergarten: Counterproductive policies. *The Elementary School Journal, 89,* 135–146.

Spodek, B. (1981). The kindergarten: A retrospective and contemporary view. Urbana, IL: Clearinghouse on Elementary and Early Childhood Education (ERIC Document Reproduction Service No. ED 206 375).

Teale, W. (1988). Developmentally appropriate assessment of reading and writing in the early childhood classroom. *The Elementary School Journal, 89,* 173–184.

Warger, C. (Ed.) (1988). *A resource guide to public school early childhood programs*. Alexandria, VA: Association for Supervision and Curriculum Development.

Zigler, E., & Valentine, J. (Eds.). (1979). *Project Head Start: A legacy of the war on poverty*. New York: Free Press.

Appendix:
A Selected Annotated Bibliography of Evaluation Instruments for Infancy and Early Childhood

1. Title: *AAMD Adaptive Behavior Scale, School Edition*
    Author(s): N. Lambert, M. Windmiller, and L. Cals
    Publisher: American Association on Mental Deficiency
    Publication Date: 1981
    Type of Test: Behavior rating scale

Uses for which the test is recommended: Assesses behavioral and affective competencies of individuals from 3 to 69 years. It is intended to be used with developmentally disabled individuals who are mentally retarded and emotionally maladjusted.

2. Title: *Bayley Scales of Infant Development*
    Author: M. Bayley
    Publisher: The Psychological Corporation
    Publication Date: 1969
    Type of Test: Infant development

Uses for which the test is recommended: Measures infant development, and includes a mental and motor scale of development. An infant behavior record also provides a systematic way of assessing and recording observations of the child's behavior when examined.

3.   Title: *Boehm Test of Basic Concepts*
     Author: A. Boehm
     Publisher: The Psychological Corporation
     Publication Date: 1986
     Type of Test: Individual or group screening test of concepts

Uses for which the test is recommended: Intended for use in kindergarten through second grade for screening and teaching. It measures knowledge of various concepts that are thought to be necessary for achievement in the first few grades of school.

4.   Title: *The Brigance Inventories*
     Author: A. Brigance
     Publisher: Curriculum Associates
     Publication Date: *Brigance Diagnostic Inventory of Basic Skills,* 1976; *Brigance Diagnostic Inventory of Early Development,* 1977
     Type of Test: Informal diagnostic and screening inventories

Uses for which the test is recommended:
     Brigance Diagnostic Inventory of Basic Skills: Designed for use with children in grades K–6 to assist teachers in adjusting curriculum and instruction for mainstreaming the handicapped.
     Brigance Diagnostic Inventory of Early Development: Designed for the developmental period from birth to 6 years. Assesses psychomotor development, self-help skills, speech and language, general knowledge and comprehension, and early academic skills.

5.   Title: *California Achievement Tests, Forms E and F*
     Publisher: CTB/McGraw-Hill
     Publication Date: 1985
     Type of Test: Norm-referenced achievement tests

Uses for which the test is recommended: To provide information for use in making educational decisions leading to improved instruction in the basic skills. Measures prereading, reading, spelling, language, mathematics, and reference skills.

6.   Title: *Denver Developmental Screening Test-Revised*
     Authors: W. Frankenburg, J. Dodds, J. Fandal, E. Kazuk, and M. Cohrs
     Publisher: University of Colorado Medical Center
     Publication Date: 1975
     Type of Test: Developmental screening

Uses for which the test is recommended: Measures development—gross motor, fine motor, language, and personal-social. Used to identify children from birth to 6 years of age with serious developmental delays.

7.   Title: *Developmental Indicators for the Assessment of Learning-Revised*
     Authors: C. Mardell-Czudnowski and D. S. Goldenberg

Publisher: Childcraft Education Corporation
Publication Date: 1983
Type of Test: Individual screening

Uses for which the test is recommended: Assesses motor, concept, and language skills for children aged 2 to 6 years. It is intended to screen the range of abilities from severe dysfunction to potentially advanced.

8. Title: *Gesell School Readiness Test*
    Authors: Gesell Institute of Human Development
    Publisher: Programs for Education
    Publication Date: 1978
    Type of Test: School readiness

Uses for which the test is recommended: Used to determine whether children are ready to begin kindergarten and to answer questions about appropriate grade placement.

9. Title: *Kaufman Assessment Battery for Children*
    Authors: A. Kaufman and N. Kaufman
    Publisher: American Guidance Service
    Publication Date: 1983
    Type of Test: Individual intelligence, achievement

Uses for which the test is recommended: Intended for use in schools and clinical settings to measure intelligence and achievement for children aged 2 to 6 through 12 to 15 years.

10. Title: *McCarthy Scales of Children's Abilities*
    Author: D. McCarthy
    Publisher: The Psychological Corporation
    Publication Date: 1972
    Type of Test: Cognitive abilities

Uses for which the test is recommended: Measures the cognitive abilities of children from 2 1/2 to 8 1/2 years. Can be used for the assessment of young children with learning problems or other exceptional conditions. Measures intellectual functioning, including verbal ability, nonverbal reasoning, number aptitude, short-term memory, and coordination.

11. Title: *Metropolitan Readiness Test*
    Authors: J. Nurss and M. McGauvran
    Publisher: The Psychological Corporation
    Publication Date: 1976
    Type of Test: School readiness

Uses for which the test is recommended: Designed to evaluate a child's readiness for school and to develop the skills necessary for success in school. Assesses readiness for formal school learning from kindergarten to early first grade.

12. Title: *Neonatal Behavioral Assessment Scale*
   Author: T. B. Brazelton
   Publisher: Education Development Center
   Publication Date: 1973
   Type of Test: Neonatal rating scale

Uses for which the test is recommended: To identify mild neurological dysfunctions and variations in temperament. Measures temperamental differences, nervous system functions, and the capacity of the neonate to interact.

13. Title: *Peabody Picture Vocabulary Test-Revised*
   Authors: L. Dunn and L. Dunn
   Publisher: American Guidance Service
   Publication Date: 1981
   Type of Test: Receptive vocabulary

Uses for which the test is recommended: Designed to evaluate the hearing vocabulary or receptive knowledge of vocabulary of children and adults.

14. Title: *Stanford-Binet Intelligence Scale* (4th ed.)
   Authors: R. Thorndike, E. Hagen, and J. Sattler
   Publisher: Houghton Mifflin
   Publication Date: 1986
   Type of Test: Intelligence

Uses for which the test is recommended: To assess the cognitive ability of young children, adolescents, and young adults. Subtests may be used to identify learning-disabled children, assess brain damage, and measure the cognitive skills of hearing-impaired children with visual-spatial or mathematical talents.

15. Title: *Wechsler Intelligence Scale for Children-Revised*
   Author: D. Wechsler
   Publisher: The Psychological Corporation
   Publication Date: 1974
   Type of Test: Intelligence

Uses for which the test is recommended: Used for clinical and psychoeducational work. Useful in the assessment of brain–behavior relationships. Intended to evaluate children's intellectual ability.

16. Title: *Wechsler Preschool and Primary Scale of Intelligence*
   Author: D. Wechsler
   Publisher: The Psychological Corporation
   Publication Date: 1967
   Type of Test: Intelligence

Uses for which the test is recommended: Assesses the cognitive abilities of preschool children and includes developmental data that can be used for program planning.

Glossary

achievement test A test that measures the extent to which a person has acquired information or mastered certain skills, usually as a result of instruction or training.

age norms Norms on standardized tests representing typical or average performance for persons in various age groups. Age norms are generally used in the interpretation of tests of mental ability.

alternate-form reliability The correlation between results on alternate forms of a test. Reliability is the extent to which the two forms are consistent in measuring the same attributes.

anecdotal record A written description of an incident in a child's behavior that can be significant in understanding the child.

aptitude test A test designed to predict future learning or performance on some task if appropriate education or training is provided.

attitude inventory An instrument that measures a person's interest in a certain area or vocation. It is not used with very young children.

attitude measure An instrument that measures how an individual is predisposed to feel or think about something (a referent). A teacher can design a scale to measure students' attitudes toward reading or mathematics.

checklist A sequence or hierarchy of concepts and/or skills organized in a format that can be used to plan instruction and keep records.

concurrent validity The extent to which test scores on two forms of a test measure are correlated when they are given at the same time.

construct validity The extent to which a test measures a psychological trait or construct. Tests of personality, verbal ability, and critical thinking are examples of tests with construct validity.

content validity The extent to which the content of a test such as an achievement test represents the objectives of the instructional program it is designed to measure.

correctives Instructional materials and methods used with mastery learning that are implemented after formative evaluation to provide alternative learning strategies and resources.

criterion-referenced test A test designed to provide information on specific knowledge or skills possessed by a student. The test measures specific skills or instructional objectives.

developmental checklist A checklist that emphasizes areas and levels of development in early childhood.

developmental screening Evaluation of the young child to determine if development is proceeding normally. It is used to identify children whose development is delayed.

diagnostic evaluation An evaluation to analyze an individual's areas of weaknesses or strengths and to determine the nature and causes of the weaknesses.

equivalent form Forms of a test that are parallel. The forms of the test measure the same domain or objectives, have the same format, and are of equal difficulty.

event sampling An observation strategy used to determine when a particular behavior is likely to occur. The setting when the behavior occurs is more important than the time it is likely to occur.

formative evaluation Evaluations conducted during instruction to provide the teacher with information on the learning progress of the student and the effectiveness of instructional methods and materials.

formative test A test designed to evaluate progress on specific learning objectives or a unit of study.

grade equivalent The grade level for which a given score on a standardized test is the esti-

mated average. Grade-equivalent scores, commonly used for elementary achievement tests, are expressed in terms of the grade and month.

grade norms Norms on standardized tests based on the performance of pupils in given grades.

graphic rating scale A rating scale that can be used as a continuum. The rater marks characteristics by descriptors on the scale at any point along the continuum.

group test A test that can be administered to more than one person at a time.

individual test A test that can be administered to only one person at a time. Many early childhood tests are individual tests because of the low maturity level of the examinees.

individualized instruction Instruction based on the learning needs of individual students. It may be based on criterion-related evaluation or diagnosis.

informal tests Tests that have not been standardized. Teacher-designed tests are an example.

intelligence quotient (IQ) An index of intelligence expressed as the ratio of mental age to chronological age. It is derived from an individual's performance on an intelligence test as compared to that of others of the same age.

intelligence test A test measuring those developed abilities considered to be a sign of intelligence. Intelligence is general potential independent of prior learning.

interest inventory A measure used to determine interest in an occupation or vocation. Students' interest in reading might be determined by such an inventory.

internal consistency The degree of relationship among items on a test. A type of reliability that indicates whether items on the test are positively interrelated and measure the same trait or characteristic.

item analysis The analysis of single test items to determine their difficulty value and discriminating power. Item analysis is conducted in the process of developing a standardized test.

learning disability A developmental difference or delay in a young or school-age child that interferes with the individual's ability to learn through regular methods of instruction.

mastery testing Evaluation to determine the extent to which a test taker has mastered particular skills or learning objectives. Performance is compared to a predetermined standard of proficiency.

mean The arithmetic average of a set of test scores.

minimum competency test A test that measures whether test takers have achieved a minimum level of proficiency in a given academic area.

multiple choice A type of test question in which the test taker must choose the best answer from among several options.

neonatologist A physician who specializes in babies less than a month old.

normal distribution The hypothetical distribution of scores that has a bell-shaped appearance. This distribution is used as a model for many scoring systems and test statistics.

norm-referenced test A test where the test taker's performance is compared with the performance of persons in a norm group.

norms Statistics that supply a frame of reference based on the actual performance of test takers in a norm group. A set of scores that represent the distribution of test performance in the norm group.

numerical rating scale A series of numerals, such as 1 to 5, that allows an observer to indicate the degree to which an individual possesses a particular characteristic.

obstetrician A physician who specializes in pregnancy and childbirth.

pediatrician A physician who specializes in the development, care, and diseases of young children.

percentile A point or score in a distribution at or below which fall the percentage of cases indicated by the percentile. The score scale on a normal distribution is divided into 100 segments, each containing the same number of scores.

percentile rank The test taker's test score, as expressed in terms of its position within a group of 100 scores. The percentile rank is the percentage of scores equal to or lower than the test taker's score.

personality test A test designed to obtain information on the affective characteristics of an individual (emotional, motivational, or attitudinal). The test measures psychological makeup rather than intellectual abilities.

psychological test A test for measuring human characteristics that pertain to observable and intraindividual behavior. The test measures past, present, or future human behavior.

rating scale A scale using categories that allow the observer to indicate the degree of a characteristic that the person possesses.

raw score The number of right answers a test taker obtains on a test.

readiness test A test that measures the extent to which a student has the prerequisite skills necessary to be successful in some new learning activity.

reliability The extent to which a test is consistent in measuring over time what it is designed to measure.

running record A description of a sequence of events in a child's behavior that includes all behaviors observed over a period of time.

scaled score The score obtained when a raw score is translated into a score that uses the normal curve for points of reference. Examples of scaled scores are IQ scores, percentiles, T scores, and Z scores.

school diagnostician A school staff member who has been trained to administer psychological tests for screening and diagnostic purposes.

school psychologist A psychologist who specializes in testing and in the learning and emotional problems of school children.

scope (sequence of skills)   A list of learning objectives established for areas of learning and development at a particular age, grade level, or content area.

specimen record   Detailed observational reports of children's behavior over a period of time that are used for research purposes.

split-half reliability   A measure of reliability whereby scores on equivalent sections of a single test are correlated for internal consistency.

standard deviation   A measure of the variability of a distribution of scores around the mean.

standard error   An estimate of the possible magnitude of error present on test scores.

standard score   A transformed score that reports performance in terms of the number of standard deviation units the raw score is from the mean.

standardized test   A test that has specified content, procedures for administration and scoring, and normative data for interpreting scores.

stanine   A scale on the normal curve divided into nine sections, with all divisions except the first and the last being 0.5 standard deviation wide.

summative evaluation   Evaluations obtained at the end of a cycle of instruction to determine whether students have mastered the objectives and whether the instruction has been effective.

summative test   A test to determine mastery of learning objectives administered for grading purposes.

T score   A standard score scale with a mean of 50 and a standard deviation of 10.

table of specifications   A table of curriculum objectives that have been analyzed to determine to what level of Bloom's Taxonomy of Educational Objectives the student must demonstrate mastery.

test-retest reliability   A type of reliability obtained by administering the same test a second time after a short interval and then correlating the two sets of scores.

time sampling   Observation to determine the frequency of a behavior. The observer records how many times the behavior occurs during uniform time periods.

true score   A hypothetical score on a test that is free of error. Because no standardized test is free of measurement error, a true score can never be obtained.

Z score   A standard score that expresses performance in terms of the number of standard deviations from the mean.

Index